THE TRIPLE GODDESS

THE TRIPLE GODDESS

1989

An Exploration of the Archetypal Feminine

By Adam McLean

Hermetic Research Series Number 1

Phanes Press
1989

92 91 90 89   4 3 2 1

Published by Phanes Press, PO Box 6114, Grand Rapids, MI 49516, USA.

Library of Congress Cataloging-in-Publication Data

McLean, Adam.
      The triple goddess : an exploration of the archetypal feminine /
by Adam McLean.
            p.   cm. — (Hermetic research series ; #1)
      ISBN 0-933999-77-1 (alk. paper) : $21.95. — ISBN 0-933999-78-X
(pbk. : alk. paper) : $10.95
            1. Goddesses.   2. Trinities.   3. Mythology—Psychological aspects.
4. Archetype (Psychology)   5. Femininity (Psychology)   I. Title.
II. Series
BL473.5.M34   1989   89-34802
291.2' 144—dc20   CIP

This book is printed on alkaline paper which conforms to the permanent paper standard developed by the National Information Standards Organization.

Printed and bound in the United States of America

Contents

Introduction 7

The Triple Goddess in Greek Creation Myths 19
    The Daughters of Night 27
        The Erinyes or Furies 30
        The Moirae or Fates 33
        The Hesperides 34
    The Daughters of the Sea Deities: The Phorcydes. 36
        The Gorgons 39
        The Graeae 41
        The Sirens 42
        The Harpies 44
    The Daughters of the Sky God 45
        The Horae 49
        The Charities or Graces 52
        The Muses 53

Demeter and Persephone 57

Hecate 66

Hera 71

The Judgement of Paris 75

Additional Examples of the Triple Goddess Found in Various Traditions 79

Suggestions and Hints for Further Research 105

Conclusion 110

INTRODUCTION

The Goddess is an eternal archetype in the human psyche. She will always be with us even though we neglect her, repress her, or outwardly deny her existence. She has shown herself to us from the earliest times of our civilization in cave drawings and primitive sculpture, in the great mythologies, and she appears in many guises in our present culture. She is part of the fabric of our being to which all humanity must inwardly relate if we are to have an inner balance in our souls. So essentially is she a part of humankind that even if in the next centuries we become children of the Cosmos, leaving Earth behind in our voyage to the stars, we will undoubtedly meet her in the dark depths of space.

Venus of Willendorf: Paleolithic Goddess Figure

In ancient times we projected her outwardly from within ourselves, saw her in the Kingdoms of Nature, within the body of the Earth, or working behind human destiny. We experienced her as a power beyond and above ourselves—a power that transformed and challenged us, as well as a being that nourished, protected and preserved us.

During this present century we have come to recognize a structure or layering of human consciousness, and we can now see that the Goddess dwells as an archetype within our inner space, as essential to us as a physical heart. Despite this, she has been so exiled to deep, hidden recesses of our soul that we often do not recognize her subtle workings, and only when she manifests in an outwardly powerful or disruptive manner do we see her at all.

The past two and a half millennia have seen the rise and domination of the soul by powerful masculine divinities who, not content with their proper

Roman Goddesses of Fate

half of the Cosmos and the human soul, usurped her place in the scheme of things, and tried to destroy her outer manifestations. Thereafter she wrapped herself in our inner soul substance and worked from within. The patriarchal religions triumphed outwardly, imposing their will upon humanity. This patriarchal period, which we can now see is coming to an end, saw the development of various abilities in the human soul: the mastery of the physical world through imperialism, the development of a material scientific tradition wedded to a technological culture, the exploitation and rape of the limited resources of the Earth, and the organization of aggression in society through nationalistic wars. We can all recognize the inheritance of this period of polarized patriarchy.

But the Goddess remained with us. While we remain human we cannot be truly separated from her. She has worked subtly through the long period of her repression, surfacing occasionally in outer history at times when we see her attributes projected onto personalities or movements in society. It would make a fascinating and informative study to trace her many appearances and the impact of her energies on the outer history of the past millennia. In many ways our patriarchal tradition has emphasized the development of consciousness via the masculine sense of grasping and mastering forces in the world and in human society. When we look at history and cannot understand a particular development in these terms, we have to recognize that another factor arises out of the inner ground of the human soul, to which the Goddess has been banished. In this way she still works within humanity, though we may be unconscious of the source of such transforming energies.

In recent years, especially since the mid-point of this century, humanity has begun to reconnect in a conscious way with the feminine side of the psyche.

Tentatively the Goddess begins to emerge again. She can be seen in a concern for the being and wholeness of the Earth under the name 'Ecology'; in the rejection of the patriarchal warmongering opposed by an emerging peace movement; in the development of 'caring' facets in our society such as social work, education and health services; and also in the recent emergence of the 'gay' community from the shadows and fringes of society, bringing with it a new sense of the integrity of individual sexuality and its more feminine orientation. The women's movement both in its political and personal developmental aspects also evidences an emerging awareness of the feminine. In all these and in many other ways, we can recognize the emergence of a new relationship of humanity with the feminine, the Goddess within our beings.

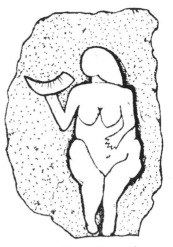

Venus of Laussel

At such a moment it is important to understand the energies and qualities of the Goddess. To take stock of the ways she can manifest within us and within the collective being of humanity, we must look at the past traditions of the Goddess, and of how she appeared in the ancient mythologies; perhaps this might better equip us to grasp her appearance in this present age. Of course, we cannot return to the old ways and recapture the past, but we can learn something regarding our present inner realities from these ancient patterns.

The ancient mythologies, being derived in part from the mystery religions and initiation traditions, projected the inner structure of the psyche outward into the world; the Gods and Goddesses were pictured as being forces in the outer realm of Nature. One of the most important developments of this century is the unfolding of a 'psychology' that recognizes the formative energies of such mythological pictures, and realizes that by contemplating the ancient mythologies we can, indeed, look at the fabric of our own souls. We in turn can breathe in the substance of these myths and come to see clearly the patterns of our own inner nature.

**Celtic Serpent Goddess
(British)**

So it is the task of this book to outline a few manifestations of the Goddess in mythology, for the purpose of providing a greater understanding of her impact and relevance to our souls today. Mythology must not be studied too abstractly or we will stand remote and detached from its substance; rather we must immerse ourselves in its stream, contemplating its symbols, meditating upon its profundities, and letting it enter our dreams and creative imaginations.

The Goddess is triple, manifesting in a threefold form, because she unites within herself the complements and the opposites of the psyche. Thus she is both gentle and caring and at the same time harsh and ruthless. She is full of light and fair visions, but simultaneously can lead one into darkness and terrible horrors.

Of course, such polarities are an essential part of the architecture of the human soul. The important thing we have to realize is the complementary nature of these polarities, of how one flows inevitably into the other and then flows back again. The polarities depend upon each other, are part of one another; through their relationships and encounters arises the dynamic energy of the psyche, the inner mercury of the soul substance that constantly moves from one pole to the other, and which, in its eternal movement, creatively discovers and explores. Without this polarity our inner life would become dried up, merely a dead husk, a fossilized realm.

The prevailing impulse of patriarchy that began to come to its ascendancy some 2000 - 3000 years ago through its denial of the feminine could not preserve a mythology that united such polarities. Instead, it sought to deny one of these poles. Thus arose the awful disease of dualism, in which the patriarchal tradition identified one polarity as 'good' and another as 'evil.' This produced a sense of an absolute 'rightness' important for such patriarchal civilizations founded upon military might and imperialism. Such a civilization could always project the image of 'evil' upon some race or people they wished to conquer, while basking all the while in its own rectitude, sure of the fact that their 'God' was on their side. Such impulses are by no means eradicated from our present world; for example, the East-West, Capitalist-Communist dualism still provides the driving energy for an absurd conflict and competition between nations and peoples.

Mythologically, the patriarchal structure could only incorporate its dualistic opposite in the form of rival deities. In this naive dualism there was a hierarchy of 'good' gods, full of light and well intentioned towards humanity, and an inverted hierarchy of 'evil' gods of the underworld, constantly plotting against humanity and trying to destroy all that the particular patriarchal religion or society stood for. Thus, during the strife between the Muslims and the Christians, each party viewed the other as 'infidel' nonbelievers, and in turn the Christian and Islamic faiths both persecuted the Jews throughout history.

Stele of Astarte at Tunis

It is obvious that a masculine mythology cannot integrate the polarities of dualism, and if we as a society were to continue to work through these archetypes we would be condemning ourselves and our descendants to the continuation of interpersonal and international struggle and conflict. On a personal level we would also be denying an opportunity for the integration of the opposites in the psyche and the corresponding release of the enormous resources of creative human energy bound up within us because of this dualism.

The feminine, however, is able to unite the opposites. Her cosmic image is the Moon, with her dark New Moon phase, her bright Full Moon phase and her intermediate waxings and wanings. She is not

11

Cretan Serpent Goddess

constant but moves through a cycle, entering the darkness and later bringing light. The male Gods, identified with the light of the Sun could not go through such a cycle; their mythologies were forced into dualism—the 'good' Sky Gods and the 'evil' Gods of the dark 'underworld'. On the other hand, the Triple Goddess bears within herself all of the polarities. We meet her in a variety of guises, and, as she is changeable, she challenges our one-dimensional thinking with contradictions and seeming inconsistencies. She shifts her shape with each turn of her cycle and our thinking must adjust to change in order for us to comprehend her.

When we relate to the Triple Goddess facet of ourselves we will initially be perturbed by her changeability. The centuries of patriarchal, rigid, one-dimensional, abstract thinking struggle against her, rejecting her impulse as 'chaotic' and leading to an inner anarchy. But as we change inwardly and the patterns of our souls mould to her formative energies we will see her more clearly. We will come to value a consciousness of cyclical change within ourselves. Once we have come to an inner relationship with the Feminine, we can begin the process of uniting the masculine and feminine facets of our souls. This, the true Mystical Marriage, the Conjunction of Opposites, is the most exciting and valuable adventure that any human being can undertake. Out of this Conjunction, this inner meeting and integration, can arise such a powerful current of creative energy as few have ever experienced. If humanity could collectively embark on this journey, great creative energy would be released, and we could render ourselves true vessels for the spiritual energies of the future.

To find the Triple Goddess in mythology we must go back to an early stratum of myth. Long before the ascendancy of the Christ myth, the primal myths of the Goddess had been overlaid with generations of masculine Gods usurping her place in the scheme of things, taking over her sacred centers and grasping for themselves some facet of her attributes. If we go back to the earliest myths of humankind we will find the Goddess in her purest, usually triune, form. In ancient Egypt it is Neith/Nut and later Isis who represent her to us. We note how the worship and recognition of Isis remains strong, although in later dynasties of Egypt there begins a masculinization of the hierarchy of Gods with Amun-Ra. In ancient Greece the earliest myths outlined many manifestations of the Goddess. Those who have studied Greek mythology can see how, probably at the beginning of the first millennium B.C., the European sky God Zeus-Dyeus was imported into Greece by a new wave of migration. From then on the character of the Greek myths changed somewhat as Zeus, through rape and cunning, deposed the Goddess from many of her centers of worship. He fathered sons upon individual Goddesses (but these sons eventually gathered to themselves some of their mothers' attributes). Thus we can see that the Greek peoples at this transition point needed to identify with male Gods rather than the older Goddess, so they rewove their mythology to suit. However, this process is quite transparent because scholars can trace such changes in the myths, and by eliminating the newer influences, recover the essence of the primal Goddesses.

Goddesses on Greek vase

Greek mythology will in fact provide us with the richest source of Goddess material. As an example of such a process, consider the God Apollo. Apollo is fathered by Zeus upon Leto, a Titan Goddess belonging to the ancient stratum of Gods and Goddesses existing in Greece before Zeus and his consort Hera. Hera is jealous of this relationship with the older Goddess and tries to prevent Leto from giving birth, but she is able to escape to a distant island. There she gives birth to Apollo and his twin sister Artemis. Apollo is a solar God and Artemis becomes the

huntress and virgin Goddess of the lunar light.
Apollo is gifted with music and many myths tell of
him as a source of inspiration, playing upon his lyre.
However, though Apollo was a popular God amongst
the Greek people, somehow he could never entirely
usurp the place of the pre-existing Muses who represented a triune form of the Goddess. The Muses
remained the feminine spiritual inspiration behind
music, poetry and the arts. We can see how the cult
of Apollo tried to replace the Muses with a masculine God, but the collective psyche of the Greek
peoples could not surrender their Goddesses of Inspiration so easily. Apollo thus had to become a
protector of the Muses rather than their rival. One
can trace many examples of such processes in which
male divinities try to replace Goddesses in early
mythologies. Greek mythology is quite transparent
in this way, probably because it was written down
while such processes were underway. Other mythologies, for example those of the Teutonic and
Scandinavian peoples, were only written down
centuries or even millennia after these processes
had been completed, and it is more difficult to
unravel the threads and identify the earlier strata of
Goddesses in those cultures.

Babylonian Seal

The triplicity of the Goddess is very important.
This is not merely a multiplying by three, but rather
a threefold manifestation; the Goddess reveals herself on three levels, in the three realms of the world
and of humankind. Thus the human being is threefold, having body, soul and spirit, and the Goddesses'
three facets are often seen as corresponding to these
realms within the microcosm of the human being.
The macrocosm is also threefold: it consists of the
heavens (Ouranian realm), the surface of the Earth
(also sometimes the Sea), and the depths of the Earth
(the chthonic Underworld). Some Triple Goddesses
have facets which link them to these three realms.
Also, the realm of time is threefold—Past, Present,
Future—and some Goddesses correspond in a three-

fold manner to the division of time.

As I have indicated above, the Triple Goddess unites dualities, so in some of her appearances one facet of the Goddess is positively inclined towards human beings who encounter her, another facet is negatively disposed, and a third facet mediates between the two and decides her course of action.

The most important triple aspect of the Goddess is her manifestation as Virgin/Mother/Crone. This is perhaps the easiest representation with whom people can identify, as this triplicity corresponds to the three phases of a woman's life. It also links us to the cycle of the Moon's phases and the female menstrual cycle, ovulation and possible impregnation. These are processes which correspond to the Young Woman/Mother/Old Woman facets.

Selene:
Triple Moon Goddess

Another way of looking at the Triple Goddess can arise through seeing her in various possible relationships with the masculine. Thus she can be seen as Virgin, having no connection with the masculine (as with Athene), as the mature and faithful wife figure (Hera), or as the Whore who chose her many lovers (Aphrodite). The Goddess can also be seen through relationships with the masculine that do not involve this sexual aspect. Thus she can be the Daughter (or sometimes Sister), the Wife and the Widow in her three facets.

The Hermetic conception of the Three Principles—Salt, Sulphur and Mercury—can also provide a picture of the three facets of the Goddess. Salt is the contractive, dark, earthly principle in the world; Sulphur is the radiating, expansive, light, heavenly principle in action; and Mercury is that which intermediates and interweaves the Salt and Sulphur of our beings. Mercury rises up into the Sulphur element and takes an essence down into the dark solidity of the Salt sphere within our soul, eternally cycling between these polarities. In this way Mercury can be seen as a picture of our consciousness, and this triplicity can be reduced, though it is a gross simplification, to the trinity of Body, Soul and Spirit in our natures. Some of the Triple Goddesses have facets which seem to parallel the triplicities of Salt, Mercury and Sulphur, or Body, Soul and Spirit, particularly in those cases where two facets of the Goddess are polarized and almost antagonistic to one another, while the third member of the triplicity mediates between them.

There are many other ways of approaching this triplicity for it provides an archetype that resonates with the inner structure of our souls, and if we meditate and work inwardly with these archetypes many further insights into the triplicity of the Goddess will unfold.

**Alchemical Illustration
(17th Century)**

This threefoldness can be followed up into many facets of life and makes the Triple Goddess an easy figure with whom to identify. She relates to the very substance of our humanity and, if we allow her space to act as a mythic figure, can inspire our souls, nourish and sustain our inner resources and transform our innermost beings.

In this book I have chosen to focus on the Triple Goddess archetype rather than on the Goddess herself. The more general archetype was often seen in mythology as threefold; thus, for example, Aphrodite was seen as Aphrodite the Virgin, Aphrodite the Wife, and Aphrodite the Whore. A similar triplicity is found in the figure of Isis as Sister, Wife and Widow of Osiris. It would be impossible in the scope of this present book to embark upon the task of cataloguing all the triple facets of the Goddess, and I have instead limited my survey to a consideration of Goddesses who display a triple form as an essential aspect of their nature. I have also focused the book upon the Western tradition and in particular the Greek myths, which provided the most rewarding ground for my study of this aspect of mythology. I do not intend that the present book be seen as an exhaustive study of the Triple Goddess, as I do not have the background in African, South American, Oceanic or Eastern Mythology to attempt such an overview. However, I trust that in the present volume I have at least sketched an outline of the Triple Goddess archetype, given some indications of how we can relate to this triplicity, and pointed to the relevance of this archetype if we are to truly understand the mysteries of our inner being.

Babylonian Cylinder Seal

I hope that I have been able to show that the Triple Goddess archetype remains a key to unlocking the store of ancient energies and spiritual wisdom bound up and repressed in ourselves. We have inherited, by being brought up in the West, the problems of a race whose collective soul has had, through millenia of inner and outer strife, deep inner wounds carved within its substance as a result of the evolution of dualistic and one sided patriarchal structures. If we, both men and women, can reconnect with the Goddess archetype in the ground of our being, she can aid in the healing of these wounds of dualism and be an agent of transcendence, opening the door in our souls to the inner meeting and marriage of our masculine and feminine components. All is within us, if we have but the courage to undertake the journey.

**Minoan Triple Goddess
with double axe and Sun and Moon**

17

THE TRIPLE GODDESS
IN THE GREEK CREATION MYTHS

Greek mythology is inherently complex because it arose organically, growing out of the soul of the Greek people over a period of two millennia. Therefore it is not surprising to find that Greek myths are enfolded layer upon layer and that these different layers are often confused by their interpenetration with one another. This is especially true of the creation myths, for in these myths many later commentators and storytellers wished to overlay other ancient myths and impose their own views of creation. During the patriarchal period and the rise of the Olympian Gods under the aegis of Zeus, brave attempts were made to reforge the mythology of Creation so that Zeus took a formative part. However, there was such a strong memory and deep feeling in the Greek soul for the earlier Gods and Goddesses, even of the spiritual powers before the cycle of the Titans, that this attempt at rewriting the creation stories failed. Although the intrusion of these later interpretations and interpolations often confused and distorted the well-formed, balanced structure of early creation myths, it is not too difficult to pull together the threads, particularly when we realize the primal importance of the Triple Goddess archetype for the Greeks. Indeed, we find her in her purest form in the ancient creation myths.

There are a number of distinct cycles of Greek creation myths: for example, the Pelasgian creation myth closely relates to the Homeric picture of creation in which Tethys and Oceanus bring the world into being from out of the sea. Another cycle, the Orphic creation myth, tells how Nyx (Night) gives birth to the Cosmic Egg. Olympian myth presents a

Orphic Egg of Creation

19

cyclical theme in which Gaia (Earth) and Ouranos (Heaven) are seen as the primal parents. These different cycles are seemingly inconsistent and one is tempted to dismiss them as independent myths with little connection to each other. However, I believe that if we examine these cycles with an awareness of the archetype of the Triple Goddess a coherent picture emerges.

The Homeric version presents Tethys as the Great Mother Goddess, the Orphics present Nyx, while the Olympian myth focuses upon Gaia as the Creatrix. These three myths unite when we recognize these three as individual facets of the one primal Triple Goddess. Hesiod in his *Theogony* even gives a myth in which these three facets emerge from the primal Chaos and Darkness:

Gaia

Tethys connected with the element of Water
Nyx connected with the darkness of Space and the element of Air
Gaia connected with the element of Earth

Each has a masculine consort:

Tethys - Oceanus
Nyx - Erebus
Gaia - Ouranos

These three facets correspond to the triple division of consciousness in humanity. Thus the Nyx facet is the dark unconscious realm, while the Gods which arise from Gaia work more in the light-filled sphere of our consciousness. The Sea is a symbol of the interface between these two domains, as it has dark depths which unite with the unconscious realm as well as its surface waves tossed with foam upon which the light can play. Thus the beings that emerge out of this facet often have a twofold nature, a light and a dark side.

20

It is instructive to look at the names of some of the children and descendants of these three streams of creation.

SEA	SKY	EARTH
TETHYS	NYX	GAIA
Styx	Moirae	Titans
Aphrodite	Doom, Fate and Death	Olympians
Metis	Sleep and Dreams	Zeus
Eurynome	Blame	Rhea
Dione	Woe and Strife	Hera
Europa	Nemesis	Demeter
Doris	Old Age	
Phorcys	Hecate	
	Erinyes	
	Hesperides	

I believe that this picture can give us a new insight into the interrelationship of these various elements in Greek mythology. Many writers who have immersed themselves in Greek myths have worked with the prevailing patriarchal impulses and archetypes that characterized the classical period. Only a few among these scholars—in particular we might mention Robert Graves and Karl Kerenyi—penetrated through to the underlying Goddess tradition upon which the patriarchal myths were grafted. It is this earlier root stock, in which the Goddesses are seen in balance with their male consort Gods, which holds a spiritual picture of the forces at work in the human soul and which is relevant to us today. The other road through classical Greek patriarchal mythology leads to the masculine and heroic Roman imperial impulse, thence to Christianity dominated by patriarchy and the denial of the feminine, and ultimately to the terrible wound of dualism which we have inherited in the Western soul. With the rise and dominance of the masculine principle in the first millennium B.C., humankind took a dangerous path as far as the health of our souls is concerned. We are beginning in this age to realize that in the depths of our souls we are neither exclusively male nor female, but that both facets contribute to our nature. To deny one of these facets, or to elevate and inflate the other, leads both to distortion and error and to the loss of the opportunity to experience the wholeness of our beings.

From each of these three creation streams arose three sets of Triple Goddesses, which in turn reflect this picture of the three realms in the human soul:

NYX	TETHYS	GAIA
Moirae	Gorgons	Horae
Erinyes	Graeae	Charities
Hesperides	Sirens	Muses

The impulse that gave rise to this present book arose out of my contemplation of the nature of these triple sets of Goddesses and their interrelationships. I am surprised that the picture that emerged for me seems not to have been articulated by other writers or commentators on the Greek myths, as there is an obvious, integral system underlying these groups. The key of the Triple Goddess opens many doors in our psyche and lets us enter into the deeper layers of our being.

The Triple Goddess' Daughters of Night—The Moirae, Erinyes and Hesperides—are connected with protecting the primal energies of life. They work within our deepest unconscious as impulses involving the question of fate, our offspring, and our immortality. The Moirae, for example, work deep within the unconscious as impulses involving the question of fate. The Erinyes protect the blood line and with fury will defend that subtle essence that we

pass on to future generations in our offspring. The
Hesperides are the guardians of our inner need for
immortality.

On the other hand, the group of Triple Goddesses
arising from the Sea realm through Phorcys are
different in character and act as guardians of the
threshold. They appear archetypally at the interface
of the conscious mind with unconsciousness. In one
sense they warn us away till we are ready to make
the inner journey safely. Thus initially they have a
fearful appearance. When we descend into the inner
depths of the unconscious it seems a perilous and
dangerous task, but behind these Triple Goddess
guardians lie other figures who will help and guide
us. What is recorded of them is only the outer
picture. When we go through these figures and
confront them, their petrifying terror changes; the
mask of the priestess is removed and she stands
before us as a guide rather than as a tormentor. From
the inside the experience of the Three Graeae, the
Gorgons and the Sirens is quite different, a fact
which is indicated in the myths where we find it
recorded that, without exception, all these terrible
figures were at one time beautiful.

From the stream of Gaia or Mother Earth, by Zeus'
coupling with three Titanesses, arose the Horae, the
Charities, and the Muses. These three sets of Triple
Goddesses are full of light, grace and inspiration for
our conscious mind. One suspects that few would
find it uncomfortable to be in their presence. They
are the custodians of the Arts (Muses), of the balancing and harmony of the Soul (Horae), and of gentility
and grace (the Charities). They live as archetypes of
beauty in the heights of our being. They stand high
above us on our inner Olympus as aspirations we can
never quite reach, never quite grasp; but from these
figures, in this elevated realm of our souls, can come
an ever-flowing stream of inspiration and creative
energy arising from a joy in life.

I believe that we should recognize all these facets in our beings as sources of inspiration. They reflect separate aspects of the Triple Goddess. To pursue one of these facets exclusively leads to an unbalanced development. Indeed, this is one criticism that patriarchy always holds up against the feminine mysteries.

If one followed exclusively the facet of the Daughters of Night, one would be led deep into dark unconsciousness and would have no harmony with other planes of one's being. One recognizes this in the excesses of the Maenads, followers of the Dionysian cult who threw themselves headlong into the unconscious.

To follow exclusively the beautiful, light-filled, gentle realm of the Muses and Graces is another error for the soul, though many people would not recognize it as such. One is in danger of becoming 'precious,' 'fay,' 'twee,' or 'pretty' when one loses a connection to one's earthly nature. This may be gentle and beautiful but is nevertheless an overwhelming problem for the feminine component of our souls. Many women with creative energies—and also sensitive men open to the feminine side of themselves—succumb to this illusory way of working with themselves, and occasion the scorn and ridicule of the more solid-footed male establishment.

Those who immerse themselves in the Phorcydes group of archetypes, the guardian Gorgons, become obsessed with the boundary, the interface, or threshold between the conscious and unconscious. They are both attracted and repelled by these archetypes and become in a sense petrified and frozen in their actions, unable to move in either direction. Such people come to feel secure only when standing in this middle ground of the soul, simultaneously skeptical and fascinated by the spiritual. They are unable to reach out to the Muses in the heights of their souls and lack the courage to penetrate through to the mysteries of their unconscious. This rigidity, inability to move, resistance to change, or fear of the new, is often leveled as a criticism of the feminine side of our nature by the patriarchal male.

So we can see that certain problems will arise for us if we attempt only to work through one facet of the Triple Goddess. These inner difficulties arising in the soul can rigidify and harden into distinct habits of personality which have been put forward as stereotyped images of woman's imperfections and inabilities by the patriarchal establishment throughout the millennia. We must come to work with all the facets of the Goddess archetype simultaneously. If we do, certain resonances will be set up between the three realms of our souls, and these will allow a communication and interchange of energies between these realms. Then the unconscious will begin to speak with our conscious mind and a dialogue will ensue. From this dialogue arises the possibility of a true healing of the soul's wounds through the inner marriage of the opposites.

THE DAUGHTERS OF NIGHT

The Daughters of Night, the Erinyes, Moirae and the Hesperides, each reflect aspects of the dark side of the Goddess. In the soul these represent primal elements of the dark unconscious part of our beings. Although we may not be in a continuous sense aware of their presence, nevertheless they do live in us as foundations within the unconscious. If we intrude upon their spheres of influence they will manifest themselves, suddenly erupting out of nowhere, appearing before our conscious gaze, sometimes projected onto people or events around us. They embody three different facets of the dark side.

The Erinyes or Furies represent the primal rage within us that hungers for vengeance after our life force has been threatened. They defend their domain by single-mindedly seeking revenge and are not interested in retribution, being quite intractable to any argument. If this primal aspect of ourselves is activated we can become focused upon vengeance, and we ourselves may be shocked at the extremes to which we might go. When such an archetype manifests collectively in society, quite monstrous deeds can be perpetrated.

The Moirae facet is much more passive, though just as unrelenting. The Moirae within us spin our fates and are an embodiment of our destinies. Contact with this aspect can either inspire or depress our life force. If we have a sense of positive currents working in our soul, through our Moirae being well disposed towards us, this can release great forces of positivity and allow resources of life energy to become available to us. But if we come to feel our Moirae have woven a tragic or empty future for us, we will be depressed and feel drained of life energy.

The Hesperides are guardian figures in our psyche and keep from us the Golden Apples of Immortality, so we rarely encounter these beings within ourselves. The Apples of Immortality represent the essence of our previous incarnations, as well as the collective essence of the eternal part of humanity. The Hesperides keep this fruit from us to protect us from its awesome power, for our consciousness would easily be swamped if suddenly presented with knowledge of our past, our immortal part that is kept safe in our unconscious. However, occasionally some of this knowledge does find its way into our conscious mind, often initially perplexing and disturbing us; it sometimes provides a source of inspiration, even changing the whole direction of our lives. The fruit of the Hesperides is extremely powerful, and their wise guardianship of its power is essential to us.

Dante and Virgil before the Erinyes in Hades.
Gustave Doré illustration to *The Divine Comedy*.

THE ERINYES OR FURIES

Erinyes

Among the most ancient of the Greek Goddesses were the three Erinyes or Furies. In all the different creation myths the Erinyes are given a place early in the scheme of things, coming long before the later male divinities of the Zeus cycle. Thus they are seen as arising together with the Titans from a union between Air and Mother Earth, or as daughters of the Earth springing from the blood of the mutilated Ouranos, according to Hesiod. Aeschylus describes them as the Daughters of Night (Nyx), while to Sophocles they were the daughters of Darkness and the Earth.

These three crones are Alecto ('unceasing in anger'), Tisiphone ('avenger of murder' or 'retaliation') and Megaera ('the jealous one'). They live in the underworld. Aeschylus describes them as awful Gorgon-like women, wearing long black robes, with snaky locks, bloodshot eyes and clawlike nails, and they are later represented as winged maidens of serious aspect, in the garb of huntresses, with snakes or torches in their hair, carrying scourges, torches or sickles.

They avenged the spilling of blood, particularly the murder of a parent and especially the murder of a mother by her son. Then they would arise out of their abode at the gates of Hades and pursue the spiller of blood till vengeance was had. No one could escape their fury. We can see them as guardians of the blood line, the forces that work through heredity. They later were seen to have three facets, which were often given separate names. As Semnae (and also Eumenides) they were the 'venerable or kindly ones'; as Dirae they pronounced 'curses' on those who transgressed against the blood line; and as Maniae or Furiae they roamed abroad in their furious vengeful aspect. They were worshipped in their sanctuary at the foot of the Areopagus Hill in Athens.

As protectors of the rights of the matriarchal blood

line, the Erinyes did not harmonize with the change to a more patriarchal society that was developing in Greece in the first millennium B.C. The Erinyes were too ancient, too deeply woven into the hearts of people, for them to be easily replaced with a group of avenging Gods or Goddesses more sympathetic to the new climate of patriarchy. The Erinyes were, however, transformed into the kindly Eumenides, and we see this most clearly expressed in the legend of Orestes and the Furies in Aeschylus' play "The Eumenides."

Erinyes pursuing Orestes

Orestes, son of Clytemnestra, killed his mother in a fury of vengeance for her murder of Orestes' father. The Erinyes, of course, pursued him tirelessly for over a year while he tried all kinds of ways to purify himself of the bloodguilt. The Erinyes could not be pacified, and Orestes was forced to seek sanctuary in the temple of Apollo. The Gods agreed to try Orestes, and the first trial by jury was held with Athene presiding over the court. The votes were tied but the casting vote was left to Athene, who voted against the punishment of the matricide. The Erinyes were furious and cried out that the Gods of the younger generation had trodden down the ancient laws and torn them out of their hands. They threatened to ravage the land by letting a drop of their own heart's blood fall onto the earth, and, as they still had power over the forces of the blood-line, they could have brought about barrenness among humankind. They were eventually pacified and reconciled to the new order when it was agreed that they be worshipped with sacrifices at a sanctuary in their honor at Athens. They were renamed the Eumenides or 'kindly ones,' taking on the name of an earlier triad of Goddesses from the underworld who pushed edible plants through the ground as gifts to humanity. They controlled the forces of growth that worked in the plant kingdom from below. They are thus distinctly feminine earth forces, as opposed to masculine forces working from above in the sunlight. They

31

also controlled forces working through the feminine in human reproduction. The Erinyes were therefore Triple Goddess guardians and protectors of the integrity of the matriarchal blood-line while the Eumenides were the Triple Goddess nourishing and tending the flow of life through the feminine. Thus we can see that these two facets came to merge during this latter period of Greek society which was given up almost entirely to a patriarchal social structure.

**Erinyes binding
Pirithous in Hades**

THE MOIRAE OR FATES

The three Moirae are the Goddess of Fate in her triple facet. The name Moira means 'part' and the three Moirae are thus associated with the three phases or parts of the moon. They were born from the great threefold Goddess Nyx, and thus belong to the earliest stratum of divinities. Even Zeus could not go against their decrees. They were known as the Spinners of Fate who spun out the days of human life as a yarn. The length of this yarn was decided entirely by them. Clotho is the 'spinner' who bore the distaff and spun the thread of life, Lachesis is the 'apportioner' to whom the thread passed as it came off the spindle to be measured against her rod, and Atropos is the 'inevitable' who snipped the thread with her shears.

In some tales they are said to live in Heaven, in a cave beside a pool from which gushes white water, and this is probably a reference to their lunar nature.

The Moirae

At the wedding of Zeus and Hera, Gaia (Mother Earth) gave Hera the tree of Golden Apples, which was later placed under the guardianship of the three Hesperides in Hera's orchard on Mount Atlas.

The Hesperides tending their apple tree around which Ladon is entwined

The three Hesperides, by name Hespere ('the evening one'), Aegle ('the luminous one'), and Erytheis ('the crimson one'), were in one tale the Daughters of Night; they arise from the earliest strata of Gods and Goddesses long before the coming of Zeus, and in other stories they are called the daughters of Atlas, or also the children of Phorcys and Ceto. Their names clearly identify them with the Sunset, and their realm lies in the far West. They guard the Tree of the Golden Apples of Immortality together with the serpent Ladon, son of Phorcys and Ceto, who is sometimes described as having three heads. In some stories, Ladon and the Hesperides are shown as mutual guardians; in other stories they are rivals set against each other. The Hesperides sing sweetly with bright voices, which has led some recorders of the myths to confuse and relate them with the Sirens. Another set of names have been given to them: Lipara ('of soft radiance'), Chryso-themis ('golden law and order') and Asterope ('star-brilliant'). A further triplet composed of Hygieia, Medousa (also the name of one of the Gorgons), and Mapsaura bring the total up to nine, the triple three, which we note as a tripling of the Triple Goddess.

The Eleventh Labor of Heracles was to fetch some of the Apples from the Garden of the Hesperides. The great masculine hero achieved this by guile rather than strength in that he asked Atlas, in this legend the father of the maidens, to fetch some fruit for him while Heracles temporarily took Atlas' burden of the heavens upon himself. Atlas readily agreed and returned with the Apples but was reluctant to take up his burden again. Heracles outwitted poor Atlas by asking him just to hold the heavens for one moment more while Heracles made a pad for his head, and then refused to take it back. When eventually Heracles returned with the Apples and they were handed to Athene, she gave them back to the Hesperides, since it was unlawful that Hera's property should pass from their hands.

THE DAUGHTERS OF THE SEA DEITIES:
THE PHORCYDES

There are three groups of Triple Goddess figures born from the ancient sea deities Phorcys and Ceto, collectively known as the Phorcydes. They exist between the interface of our conscious and our unconscious minds just as the surface of the sea mediates between the dark realm in its depths and the light filled upper world under the vault of the sky. These three groups are guardians of this interface.

The Gorgons with their terrible masks seem to warn us against immersing ourselves prematurely in the dark depths of our psychic underworld, our unconscious realm. If we do intrude upon this realm before proper preparation, we may become petrified, have our will frozen, and become unable to comprehend the forces and awesome powers of our unconscious. We would then be reduced to complete inactivity of the soul.

The Sirens work in an opposite sense through actively trying to attract us into this sphere with their alluring song and beauty of form.

The Graeae sit at this boundary and mark its existence, but have no power to ward us off, nor do they wish to attract us into its influence. These two facets of the Graeae are remembered in myth as being not only repulsive Gray Old Women but also as having a beautiful swan-like form. The swan, being a bird which spends most of its life upon the surface of water, is a universal symbol of consciousness resting upon and being buoyed up on the deep waters of unconsciousness.

We can see that these three groups, working at the

boundary between consciousness and unconsciousness, can be distinguished from each other. The Gorgons wish to repel us and scare us off, the Graeae merely mark the boundary, and the Sirens wish to attract us and have us step into our unconscious realm whether or not we are prepared for it. The Harpies bear a relationship to the Sirens and are often confused with them in later legends and stories, and I therefore have included them in this category.

Perseus cutting off the head of Medusa

THE GORGONS

The three Gorgons lived at the far western edge of the world and their sanctuary bounded on the realm of Night. These sisters, immortal daughters of Phorcys and Ceto, were called Medusa ('the cunning one') who was mortal, Stheino ('strong') and Euryle ('wide roaming').

Originally the Gorgons had great beauty of face and form and graceful golden wings arched above their shoulders. Medusa occasioned the wrath of Athene by making love to Poseidon (the dark god of the Sea) in one of Athene's sanctuaries. Thus Athene rendered her mortal and transformed her and her

**Terrible mask form
of the Gorgon**

sisters into ugly hags, the Grim Ones. They had lizard-like scaly skin and hissing snakes for hair; their tongues protruded between boar-like tusks. Medusa was singled out as the most ugly and petrifying of the three. The terrible gaze of the Gorgons was so intense that it turned mortals to stone, and all around the cavern where they dwelt could be seen the stony figures of men and animals which had chanced to catch a glimpse of them and had been petrified by the sight. We can see them in this regard as guardian figures, protectors of the boundaries of primal ancient mysteries, guardians of the threshold. Robert Graves, among others, suggests that Gorgon masks may have been worn by priestesses at celebrations of the Mysteries to frighten away the uninitiated. Gorgon heads in the form of grotesque carvings were often placed on the walls of Greek cities to terrify their enemies, an example of the protection of boundaries which the Gorgon archetype incorporates.

The later masculine mythology tells of the hero Perseus, who, being sent on a suicide mission to obtain the head of Medusa, attracts the sympathy and aid of the Goddess Athene. With her help and the loan of winged sandals, a helmet of invisibility, and

**The 'Strozzi' Medusa:
the beautiful aspect
of the Gorgon**

a bright shield, Perseus comes to the realm of the Gorgons. Finding them asleep, he creeps up to them safe under his helmet of invisibility, and, walking backwards, looks only at the reflection of Medusa's head in the shield. With his sword guided by Athene, he is able to decapitate Medusa and escape. He brings the head of Medusa safely stowed in a magic wallet and presents it to Athene. She wore it upon her belt; or in some tales she had it fixed as the center boss of her shield.

In another myth involving the Gorgons, Athene gave two phials of Medusa's blood to Asclepius. Revered as the founder of medicine, Asclepius was skilled in surgery and the use of drugs. He used the blood from Medusa's left side to raise the dead; blood from the right side of her body caused instant death. Asclepius of course chose to work only with the curative ability of drugs. However, the fact that the Medusa's blood had both the power to kill and the power to cure demonstrates that the Medusa or Gorgon figure was not strictly negative and destructive, but had balanced within herself positive healing forces.

THE GRAEAE

The three Graeae are described as beautiful and swan-like though gray haired from birth, but some tales of these 'Three Gray Ones' represent them as ugly; reportedly they had only one eye and tooth which they passed around and shared between them. They were daughters of Phorcys and Ceto. Their names were Enyo ('warlike') who was always clothed in yellow; Pemphredo ('wasp') who was always beautifully attired; and Deino ('the terrible').

They enter little into the Greek myths that have come down to us, but they appear as guardian figures, the ones who know the way to the realm of their sisters, the Gorgons.

In the later hero myths, which glorify the masculine side of humanity, Perseus visits them at their thrones on Mount Athos to discover the way to the Gorgons. He shamelessly takes advantage of them by stealing their single eye as the sisters passed it around in order to see him. Thus Perseus is able to bargain for the information he needs, and they tell him to go to the Stygian Nymphs. From these nymphs Perseus obtains winged sandals, a magic wallet, and a helmet of invisibility; with these he is able to travel to the realm of the Gorgons, decapitate Medusa, and bring her head back to Athene.

THE SIRENS

The Sirens were sometimes described as the three daughters of the River Achelous and were said to lure sailors to their death by the charm of their voices. The name 'sirens' is derived from a Greek root meaning 'to bind or attach.' These sea nymphs were usually three in number, though different authors have given them different names. In one story they are called Aglaophonos ('of the brilliant voice'), Thelxepia ('of the words which enchant'), and Molpe ('song'). In Italy they were named differently as Parthenope ('virgin'), Leucosia ('white Goddess'), and Ligeia ('bright-voiced'). Another source names them as Thelchtereia ('enchantress'), Aglaope ('glorious face') and Peisinoe ('seductress').

A Siren

They were at first represented with the head and breasts of a woman and the body of a bird, but later were depicted as women whose bodies terminated in fish-tails.

They were said to have been the playmates of Persephone before she was abducted by Hades, after which they sought for her in vain over the whole earth. After Persephone became Queen of the Underworld, the Sirens remained servants of this death queen and were charged with bringing souls to her. This they did by luring mariners through the entrancing power of their song to destruction on the rocks below their coastal meadow.

Their thrice three names link them with the nine Muses. In one legend it is accounted how they challenged the Muses to a singing contest. The Muses won this battle and pulled out their wing feathers to make themselves victory crowns. Thus from this time the Sirens took the form of fish-women or mermaids rather than their earlier bird-women form, and were exiled to the shores of remote islands. In this myth we can see a picturing of the two facets of being carried away by the intuition, 'on the wings of song' in a sense. The Muses represent the positive aspect which gives rise to life promoting creative energies and inspiration, while the Sirens show us the negative self-destructive element that can come about by blindly following intuitions and inspirations. This will be familiar to us when we think of those artists and creative people who destroy themselves through following such phantom voices, led astray by the Sirens that still live in our psyche. Others, however, can use this inner intuition more positively, and a torrent of creative energies seems at times to pour through them. In a sense these souls are able to make a relationship with their intuition through the Muses.

The hero Odysseus on his return from Troy outwitted the Sirens through the aid of the enchantress Circe. She told him to stop the ears of his sailors with wax and have himself bound to the mast by his crew if they were to sail past the island of the Sirens in safety. Later, when the ship of the Argonauts sailed past their island, the Sirens again tried to wield the entrancing power of their voices and make the sailors jump overboard to their destruction, but this time Orpheus who was with them tuned his lyre and began to sing. The beauty of his voice countered and overcame that of the Sirens, and from that moment they lost all their power and were turned into rocks. This late myth shows the masculine triumphing over and replacing the earlier primal Triple Goddess.

Odysseus hears the call of the Sirens

THE HARPIES

**Detail from the
Harpy Monument
(British Museum)**

The word Harpy implies 'robber,' 'spoiler,' or 'snatcher.' These beings were depicted with the bodies of birds and the heads of women, and were sometimes confused with the Sirens. However, they seem to be more connected with the airy element, and have been described as personifications of the storm winds. In earlier legends they are seen as Goddesses with beautiful locks, swifter than the winds or birds in their flight. Later myths picture them as hateful and repulsive creatures, having bird bodies with the faces of old women, the ears of bears, crooked talons and hanging breasts. The three Harpies of the earlier legend are named Aello ('howler'), Celaeno ('screamer') and Ocypete ('swift').

In the legend of the Argonauts, Jason and his company visit Phineas while searching for the Golden Fleece. Phineas, who was gifted with prophesy, had been blinded by the Gods for revealing the future too accurately. He was also plagued by two Harpies, loathsome winged female creatures. At every meal they flew into his palace and stole food from his table while befouling the rest and making it inedible. In return for his advice on how to win the Golden Fleece, Phineas asked that they first rid him of the Harpies. This proved an easy task for the heroic masculine principle represented by Jason's companions, Calais and Zetes. These winged sons of Boreas the North wind quickly routed the Harpies, who returned to the depths of the earth under the island of Crete.

THE DAUGHTERS OF THE SKY GOD

Zeus, the sky-god, fathered three sets of Triple Goddess upon ancient Titan Goddesses. His off-spring were the Graces, the Horae and the Muses, and these are all aspects of the Goddess working within the sphere of our consciousness.

Zeus

The Charities or Graces are the attendants of Aphrodite; they dress her, adorn her, and make her attractive, and in this sense they are passive, reflecting existing beauty and revealing it in its full glory. The Graces work archetypally in us as powers that foster impulses toward beauty and fullness of expression. We find the Graces in our consciousness whenever we try to fashion a work of beauty from our inner selves and manifest it outwardly in the world.

The Horae represent the Seasons; they are Goddesses of the right moment, and we encounter them whenever we try consciously to bring about something in the world through our inner inspiration and energies. Sometimes we find that we are not in harmony with the Seasons, and the time is not right for such a thing to emerge through us. Difficulties often arise from our untimely expression of this aspect of ourselves; we seem then to be working against the stream. However, at another time there seems to be no such opposition to expression, and indeed we even gain help from some inward source. We stand at the right moment, and in this sense the Horae are with us; being in harmony with them we have their aid and support.

The Muses work to inspire us. They constantly live just behind the flickering images and ever tumbling thoughts that form the fabric of our consciousness. If we are attentive, if we prepare ourselves and have a positive inner attitude, then the Muses will constantly put before us inspiring pictures and ideas that we can weave and work creatively through our conscious mind. Thus if we cultivate a relationship with our inner Muses, we will rarely be short of inspiration. This fountain and inner spring of intuition and inspiration can press its creative fund of ideas and images so hard upon us that artists and creative people often find themselves swamped and overwhelmed by its stream.

This triplicity of the young woman facet of the Goddess working in our consciousness shows the Graces as passive adorners, the Horae as mediating the right moment for an idea or inspiration to come to fruition, while the Muses are the active inspiring facet behind our conscious thoughts and inner pictures.

The Realm of Zeus

First row: Zeus, Melpomene, and Thalia
Second row: Clio, Calliope, Erato, and Euterpe.
Third Row: Terpsichore, Urania, Polyhymnia, Apollo Musagetes, Delphic Priestess,
and Poet.
Fourth Row: The habitable Earth and Time, Homer supported by the Iliad and
Odyssey, the Genuis of Myth, History, Poetry, Tragedy, Comedy, Nature, Virtue,
Memory, Faith, and Wisdom.

The three Horae with Pan

THE HORAE

The word Hora means 'the correct moment' and indicates that this triplicity of Goddesses had command over cycles. Thus they were guardians of the natural order, of the yearly cycle of plant growth, the seasons, and they also ruled the cycles of the weather. Indeed, our own word 'hour' is derived from this Greek root.

They were born from the union of Zeus and Themis. It was the Moirae that brought the heavenly Themis ('order') to Zeus on Mount Olympus to be his first wife. She bore the three Horae, who were entrusted with the guardianship of the Gates of Heaven and Olympus. These three Seasons were named Eunomia ('lawful order'), Dike ('justice'), and Eirene ('peace'), and were depicted as young maidens with lovely hair, golden diadems and a light footstep, holding in their hands the products of the various seasons—a branch in flower, an ear of corn, and a vine stock. They were often associated with deities connected with the growth of vegetation. For example, they are often shown in procession with Pan. The Horae also presided at the birth of Dionysus, which occurred when he sprang from the thigh of Zeus. They were the first to receive Aphrodite new born from the waves and clothed her with a robe. Hera received their services as nurses and handmaidens.

In Athens the Horae were at one time perceived as being two in number. One was named Thallo ('sprouting') and the other Carpho ('withering'); they reflected the two forces at work in the cycles of nature. Later they became the Four Seasons, and under Alexandrian influence were seen as the daughters of Helios and Selene, Sun and Moon. Subsequent to this they were represented as twelve separate entities and were linked with the hours of the day. However, their earliest appearance was as a Triple

Two Horae

Goddess whose attributes brought about harmonization and peace among the primal polarized energies which drove the cycles of the seasons. Their domain of influence was also extended into the human soul, where they brought about a similar harmonization of the warring forces of the human psyche.

Dike, who, as her name implies, sought to encourage a just relationship between the polarities, grew so weary of the constant warring of humankind that she later withdrew from the human sphere. She moved to the mountains to await a more peaceful and just climate in the affairs of humanity. However, as the ages passed, events seemed to grow worse. Finally Dike, losing hope for humanity, withdrew altogether from the Earth and ascended to heaven to become the constellation Virgo.

The Charities or Graces. Engraving by Gustave Doré.

The three Graces were born from the union of Zeus and Eurynome, the daughter of Oceanus, one of the primeval Gods. They were 'the joyful ones,' the ever-youthful companions and handmaidens of Aphrodite. They exuded a delight in life and an enjoyment of art, dance, music and love. The names of the Graces were Thalia ('she who brings flowers'), Aglaia ('brilliance and splendor'), and Euphrosyne ('joy and mirth'). They possessed grace of movement, for they were Goddesses of the dance; grace of manners, for they were always gentle, charming and polite; and the grace of love. They tended and adorned Aphrodite when she set out on her seductions, dressing her and arranging her hair.

The Graces were often represented as a naked group in which two of them face towards the onlooker while the third shows her back. The sanctuary where they were particularly worshipped, Orchomenos in Boeotia, had three stones which were reputed to have fallen from heaven—meteorites or aeroliths.

A Greek proverb tells of how the first cup of wine at a banquet belonged to the Graces, the second to the lustful Aphrodite, while the third was ruled by the Goddess Ate, who was the embodiment of folly, moral blindness, infatuation, discord and mischief.

THE MUSES

The Greek Goddesses of art and inspiration are still relevant to us today because they connect us to important archetypes which can still be experienced by those creative individuals who look within their souls for the source of inspiration. The Muses were born as a result of the union of Zeus and Mnemosyne ('Memory'). For nine nights they lay together. After the year passed Mnemosyne gave birth to nine daughters at a place not far from the summit of Mount Olympus. They were raised there by the hunter Crotus, who was transported after death into the sky as the constellation Sagittarius. The choir of Muses made their birthplace a special dancing ground and sanctuary. They also frequented Mount Helicon, where two springs, Aganippe and Hippocrene, had the virtue of conferring poetic inspiration upon those who drank their waters. Beside these fountains the Muses would trace the graceful figures of a dance with tireless feet, while displaying the harmony of their brilliant voices.

The names and attributes of these nine sisters were as follows:

Clio ('fame-giver') was the Muse of History, and her symbols were the heroic trumpet and the clepsydra, an ancient water clock. She was often depicted with a half-opened scroll or a chest of books.

Euterpe ('joy-giver') presided over Lyric Poetry, and her symbol was the flute.

Thalia ('the festive') was the Muse of Comedy and wore the comic mask and wreaths of ivy. She is sometimes shown as carrying a shepherd's staff.

Melpomene ('the singer') was the Muse of Tragedy, and wore the tragic mask and vine leaves. She carried the club of Heracles, and was the opposite to Thalia.

Terpsichore ('she who loves dancing') was the

**The Muses:
Cards from the
Tarocchi of Mantegna**

53

Muse of Lyric Poetry and the Dance. She also ruled choral song and carried the lyre or cithara.

Erato ('awakener of desire') was the Muse of erotic verse or Love Poetry.

Polyhymnia ('many hymns') was the Muse of Sacred Hymns and later of the Mimic Art and Storytelling. She was usually depicted as veiled, in an attitude of meditation, with a finger on her mouth.

Urania ('heavenly') was the Muse of Astrology and her symbols were the celestial globe and compass.

Calliope ('beautiful voiced'), first in rank among her sisters, was the Muse of Epic Poetry and Eloquence. Her symbols were the tablet and pencil stylus.

The Muses were represented as young women with faces smiling, grave or thoughtful according to their function, dressed in long flowing robes, covered with a mantle. At an earlier time they were worshipped in threefold form. On Mount Helicon they were originally known as Melete ('practicing'), Mneme ('remembering'), and Aoide ('singing'). There were also three Muses at Sicyon and Delphi—Nete, Mese and Hypate—personifying the three strings of the lyre.

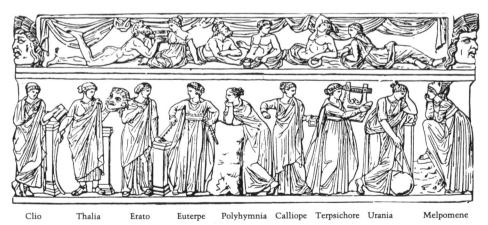

Clio   Thalia   Erato   Euterpe Polyhymnia Calliope Terpsichore Urania   Melpomene

The Muses

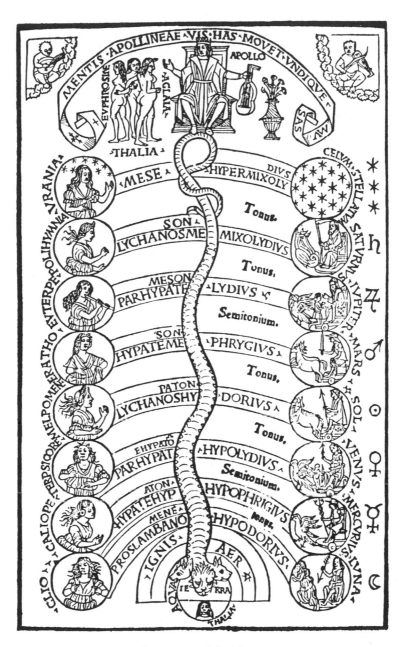

The Harmony of the Spheres:
Renaissance engraving showing the planetary spheres, musical ratios and
modes, and the nine Muses.

Demeter and Persephone

DEMETER AND PERSEPHONE

The myth of Demeter and Persephone, which lay at the heart of the Eleusinian Mysteries, provided a parallel between the inner evolution of the soul through cyclic development and the outer cycle of the seasons. These Mysteries laid down a pattern in the collective soul of Western humanity which later found expression in nature mysticism and can indeed, even today, still act as the inspiration for a certain path of inner development.

The mystery that underlies the Demeter-Persephone myth is a chthonic one concerned with our relationship to the forces of the Earth—the cycling energies that arise out of the Earth, 'the green fuse that drives the flower,' producing the germination and growth of plants. Demeter was earlier 'Ge-Meter,' i.e., the Earth Mother who unfolds herself in the growth of vegetation in the cycle of the seasons. She was particularly connected with grain as a Corn Goddess.

In this Mystery, Demeter unfolds as a Triple Goddess, her three facets being Demeter, Persephone and Hecate; each facet reveals itself at different stages of the cycle. The Demeter facet represents vegetative forces above ground level, the ripened grain, the swollen fruits of the Earth. Her Hecate aspect is seen in the dark chthonic forces, immanent, stirring deep within the earth. Persephone is the aspect that mediates between these two realms, who must belong to both realms. She is the seed that must be sown, that bears the archetypal energy of vegetation.

The myth records the development of a dynamic relationship among the three facets. At the beginning of the story there is a duality—the above ground facet and the below ground aspect of the Underworld both wish to exclusively possess the Kore, or Child, Persephone. The masculine side of the Underworld forces, Hades, carries away the Kore, and through this act of rape steals her from Demeter. The myth, which has all the elements of drama, shows that the solution to this conflicting dualism lies in a cyclical unfolding of the three facets of the Triple Goddess. This triplicity supersedes and heals the duality, mediating between the realm above the Earth and the realm of the Underworld.

These mythic events can be experienced as spiritual exercises which allow human beings to develop a healthy relationship to their unconscious selves. Indeed, this was the task set before the initiates of the Mysteries of Eleusis in the form of a sacred dramatic ritual enactment. At present, most of us have a dualistic relationship to the conscious/unconscious split in our beings. The self, the seed of our being, is either in the forefront focus of our consciousness, or deeply asleep in the sphere of our unconsciousness. A dualism arises from the inner struggle of each facet to possess the self. We all, of course, know this very well through the cycle of our waking and sleeping. If we worked in the spirit of the Demeter-Persephone mythos, as Eleusinian initiates in a sense, we would come to experience our being not as polarized into conscious/unconscious, upper world/underworld, but as a plant growing at the interface of these two realms and mediating between them, allowing a flow of energy from below to above and in the opposite direction, which is the basis of a relationship.

Now we will outline in synopsis this myth which is best recounted in the *Homeric Hymn to Demeter*.

One day Persephone was playing on the meadows of Nysa with the daughters of Oceanus. She was accompanied by Athene and Artemis but her mother,

Demeter, was not with them. Persephone was attracted by a magnificent narcissus. As she gazed at it the ground beneath her opened and Hades, the God of the Underworld, appeared on his chariot, seized hold of the maiden, and carried her away to be his bride. From far away Demeter heard her plaintive cries. Bitter sorrow seized her heart, and, throwing a sombre veil over her shoulder, she flew like a bird over land and sea seeking here and there for her Kore, her daughter. For nine days and nights she searched the world bearing torches in her hands, but no living thing could tell her what had happened to Persephone. Finally she sought the advice of Hecate, who had herself overheard the rape. Hecate suggested they consult the all-seeing Sun God Helios. Helios told them that Hades had taken away Demeter's daughter, and that Zeus himself had allowed the act.

Demeter of Cnidus

In rage Demeter withdrew from Olympus and sought refuge in the world of mankind. In the guise of an old woman, she came eventually to the city of Eleusis, and sat down beside the Well of the Virgin, immersed in her grief. There she was met by Celeos, the daughter of the King of Eleusis, who, without recognizing her as the Goddess, invited her to stay in their house. She was received by the Queen of Eleusis, Metaneira, who gave Demeter charge over her son Demophoön, heir to Eleusis. The Goddess decided to make him immortal, and annointed him with ambrosia; each night she passed him through the flames, in order to burn away his mortal nature. One night, Metaneira, though pleased with the care Demeter was taking of her child, chanced to look in upon her nurse and charge. The Queen was shocked when she saw her child in the flames, and cried out, interrupting the process undertaken by Demeter. Demeter revealed her true nature to the Queen and scolded her, saying that she would have made Demophoön eternally young, but now he must remain mortal. She asked that Metaneira and her people erect a great temple to her honor at Eleusis. In exchange she would teach the Queen sacred rites so that in the future the people of Eleusis might offer her worship to comfort her soul for the loss of her own daughter.

The temple was built and for a whole year Demeter sat mourning for her daughter within its precincts. Remote from the realm of the Gods, she also withdrew her energies from the Earth. It was a dreadful year she sent upon the all-nourishing Earth, for in the absence of her energies nothing could grow, no seed could sprout, and the oxen drew the ploughs upon the fields in vain. She would have eventually destroyed all mankind with famine, and as the Gods would thus have received no sacrifices or worship, Zeus realized that he would have to do something about this turn of events. He sent the beautiful Iris as messenger to the temple. There she found Demeter, swathed in dark raiment and impervious to entreaty. One by one the Gods and Goddesses came to her, but she still remained unmoved by their pleas. She would not set foot within the palace on Olympus, nor would the Earth bear fruit, until she was reunited with her daughter.

Realizing the extreme seriousness of matters, Zeus sent Hermes into the darkness of the Underworld to try to persuade Hades to part with his new found Queen. Hades eventually agreed to let Persephone return to the upper world, but tricked her by secretly putting into her mouth a seed of the pomegranate. Having thus eaten of the fruits of the Underworld, Persephone must of necessity return to that dark realm. Hermes took Persephone back to the upper world in his chariot, and she was reunited with her mother. (In another version of the tale it is told that it was the Moirae, the Horae and the Charities, as a band of nine dancers, that led Persephone out of the Underworld.) Demeter immediately asked her if she had eaten any food from the land of Hades. When she

Demeter, Persephone and Triptolemus

told of the pomegranate seed that Hades had secretly placed in her mouth, Demeter realized that Persephone could only remain with her for two thirds of the year and that she would have to spend the remaining third with Hades in the Underworld. She accepted this as inevitable and allowed her energies to flow upon the Earth again, permitting the corn to grow and ripen, and the Earth to be fertile. Finally, before returning to Olympus, Demeter taught the Kings of Eleusis the secrets of her divine science and initiated them into her Mysteries.

There are a number of triple facets to this myth that throw light upon the meaning of the tale. Let us first examine the Three Goddesses in the opening scene sporting themselves in the meadows of the Nysaean fields. They are Athene, Artemis and Persephone—three Virgin Goddesses. These are the Virgin facet of the Goddess further split (we have already noted how the Triple Goddess can split her three facets in a further threefold manner and thus become ninefold).

The nature of the three facets is complementary; although they all share this element of virginity, it is very different in each case.

In Athene's case, virginity can be seen as arising out of her virago nature, her incorporation of the masculine within herself. Athene does not need contact with the masculine. She personifies the wisdom facet of the Goddess.

Artemis' virginity is somewhat different. She is the wild virgin of the hunt, the feminine immersion in the unrestrained forces of wild nature. Only by remaining aloof from contact with the masculine can she retain her independence. If she were to become restrained, tamed, she would lose that wild exuberance that is the very essence of her being. Her virginity is essential to her and she guards it fiercely as the source of her independent spirit. The Greek

Artemis, to whom I refer here, should be distinguished from Artemis of Ephesus, 'Great Diana of the Ephesians,' who was the great Mother Goddess of the Ionian Greeks. The Greek soul was in later patriarchal times unhappy with the independent feminine archetype of Artemis, and encouraged the grafting onto her of the Artemis of Ephesus-Mother facet. Thus a confusion arises in many later myths as to the nature of Artemis; however, in the early myth of Demeter-Persephone we are dealing entirely with the earlier Artemis archetype.

Persephone's virginity is of a different order again. It is the virginity of innocence. We perceive this when we picture her playing on the Nysaean field, fascinated by the plant kingdom. As she looks at the hyacinths and narcissi in an innocent manner, Hades rises out of the Earth and carries her away to his kingdom to make her Queen of the Underworld. Demeter grieves for her lost child, the Kore, the facet of herself that has been lost. She discovers from Hecate that her Kore has been taken away. We see here that the myth reveals the three facets of the Triple Goddess, Demeter-Persephone-Hecate. Demeter is the Goddess of the expression of the nature forces outwardly expanding upon the surface of the Earth, the Goddess of the standing Corn. Hecate is the Triple Goddess in the Underworld, the female keeper of the forces under the Earth. Hecate is often pictured in Greek mythology and by later commentators as an awful hag, the personification of the horrors of Hell. However, there is a lighter side of her nature to which the Greeks related, that is connected to her guardianship of the Underworld. Hecate alone among the Gods and Goddesses is allowed by Zeus to have power in the three realms— the Sky, the Sea and the Earth. Because she has this lighter side and is an offspring of the Titans, she is not entirely given up to the Underworld forces and cannot be considered by Hades as a Queen of the Underworld. She is, rather, a mediator, an archetypal Moon Goddess. Of the three facets mentioned here, she is the one who can move between dark and light.

Hecate thus plays an important role in the sacred drama, pointing Demeter to the whereabouts of Persephone. (Interestingly, the author of this tale introduces the number nine at this point—Demeter searches nine days for Persephone before meeting with Hecate.) At the conclusion of the myth, Hecate is made a guardian for Persephone during her stay in the Underworld. Thus Persephone lives a part of her life united with the Demeter facet and another part in contact with the Hecate aspect, thereby becoming the archetypal mediator between the light-filled upper world and the dark underworld.

As I have indicated earlier, this myth contains a complex interlinked series of triple manifestations of the Goddess. Another triplicity I would like to draw the reader's attention to is Artemis-Persephone-Hecate. Artemis and Hecate were often seen as being manifestations of the same Goddess. Some interpreters even go so far as to refer to this figure as Artemis-Hecate. This association arises out of their having many points in common, both being Goddesses of the wild places, 'working from a distance upon humanity,' both being appointed guardians of the roads and byways, and both being associated with the dog.

The myth of Demeter and Persephone is one of the most archetypal of all myths, and I doubt whether it is not to be found, in some form, in the spiritual traditions of all the peoples of the Earth. As we have seen, it is a myth that brings before us the relationship of the forces in Nature, and thus, of necessity, will arise in the souls of those who relate themselves to the forces of the natural world. All societies in their early agricultural phases touched upon this archetype. In a sense it lies behind all paganism—'pagan' in the Roman sense means 'country-person'—and the European folk customs of medieval

Demeter
(Roman painting)

times can be seen quite clearly to express these archetypes. Medieval witchcraft was most likely to have been a naive form of celebration of such pagan mysteries, rather than some 'spiritual conspiracy' against the organized Church, which almost hounded it out of existence. During the period of the witch-craft persecutions, the Hecate figure was projected onto the women who took part in these simple country customs while the men had the Pan arche-type projected onto them as a kind of 'devil' figure. Thus it was that the patriarchal establishment of the church felt itself to be quite within its rights, indeed having the full acquiescence of the Father God, to persecute and destroy what they saw, through their projections, to be figures of evil. Perhaps what the Church most especially feared in these remnants of the Demeter-Persephone-Hecate mysteries was the Triple Goddess who challenged their dualistic view of the world.

Hades and Persephone as King and Queen of the Underworld

HECATE

Hecate as an archetype has been much misunderstood over the millennia. She is a Triple Moon Goddess connected with the dark aspect of the lunar disc. As I have shown earlier, the development in the later classical period of patriarchal society gave rise to a dualistic view of spiritual forces which warred against each other. Hecate was a prime target to be made into a figure of evil and, regrettably, this taint of uncanny evil, eldritch horror and negativity still clings to this archetype. This perception of her was especially welded into the Western psyche during the medieval period, when the organized Church projected this archetype onto simple pagan country people pursuing their ancient fertility customs and folk crafts. They were seen as evil 'devil' worshippers, as covens of witches led by ugly hags, practicing abominable rites and ceremonies in the wild countryside. Hecate appeared then as a Goddess of the witches, a patroness of the hag aspect, but it is impossible to get a clear picture of her nature due to the distorted projections, inner fears, and spiritual insecurities of obsessed 'Christian' priests and confessors.

Hecate fighting the Giants

In earlier times, before this patriarchy had fully established itself, it is easier to discover and relate to the inner essence of the Hecate archetype. She is connected with the darkness and the dark half of the Moon. The Moon, in fact, has no light of her own, being a dark planet. The light that comes from the Moon is reflected sunlight. Thus the full Moon is the Moon seen through the light of the Sun; the dark new Moon is, in a sense, the Moon's true face. Hecate is often seen as a part of a Triple Moon

Goddess—Artemis (Full Moon), Selene (Moon in various phases), Hecate (dark face of the New Moon)—or as the Moon forces in various realms: Selene in Heaven, Artemis on the Earth, Hecate in the Underworld. Interestingly, Artemis is the sister of Apollo. This links her directly with the solar forces. Artemis and Hecate are often seen as complementary facets, and in later times they were often confused with each other.

Hecate is an ancient Goddess from an earlier pre-Greek strata of myth. The Greeks found her difficult to fit into their scheme of Gods, but eventually came to see her as a daughter of the Titans Perses and Asteria, and thus cousin to Artemis. Other traditions saw her as an even more primal Goddess, making her a daughter of Erebus and Nyx. Zeus gave her a special place among the Gods, in that, although not a part of the Olympian company, she was allowed dominion over the Sky, the Earth and the Underworld; she is therefore the bestower of wealth and all the blessings of everyday life. In the human sphere she presided over the three great mysteries of birth, life and death. Her name means 'the distant or remote one,' and she was seen as the protectress of remote places, a guardian of roads and byways, and her triple nature made her especially present where three roads converged. At such places the ancient Greeks could easily meet with Hecate and consequently they kept such places sacred, often erecting three-faced statues called Hecataea. They also left offerings of her ritual food, 'Hecate's supper,' at such crossroads during her special festivals.

Hecate symbolically bore the triple nature of the Goddess in that she is usually shown with three heads (in later times often depicted as Dog, Snake and Lion), and six arms which bear three torches. Her three sacred symbols are the Key, as she was guardian wardress of the Underworld; the Scourge, revealing her punitive side, and her role of herding

The Hecaterion of Marienbad

souls in the Underworld; and the Dagger, symbol of her ritual power, which later became the Athame of the 'witches.'

In the Underworld, Hecate is the wardress and conveyor of souls, the Prytania, the 'Invincible Queen' of the Dead. After they have passed the triple-headed Cerberus and been judged by the three Judges of the Dead—Minos, Rhadamanthys, and Aeacus—souls must come to the triple crossroads of Hell. At this juncture Hecate sends them to the realm for which they are judged fit: to the Asphodel Meadows, to Tartarus, or to the Orchards of Elysium.

Hecate is a threefold Moon Goddess connected with the feminine in independence from the masculine. While both Artemis and Hecate are invoked in childbirth, this is in the sense of helping with an exclusively feminine mystery. The Triple Goddess connected with the other side of the Moon's nature, the Hera facet, is guardian of the relationship of woman to man. Thus Hera is the jealous guardian of marital fidelity, the protectress of the marriage vows. She is the Goddess of childbirth, not as a feminine ritual, but as the result of male-female connection as it relates to the preservation and integrity of the blood line and inheritance.

The Artemis-Hecate archetype was rather feared by the patriarchs because, if pursued by women, it could lead to their developing a sense of an independence from the masculine. Thus the cult of Hera under the protection of Zeus became very important in late classical times.

Today we can relate to Hecate as a guardian figure in our unconsciousness, holding the key to the dark realms within us and bearing torches to light our way into the depths of our inner being. Our patriarchal civilization has perhaps taught us to fear this figure, this terrible hag, but if we trust in her ancient energies we will find her a kindly guardian. She

stands at the triple crossroads that exist at all levels
of our being, manifesting as spirit, soul and body. We
should recognize that the terrible, awful, hag-like
image of Hecate is merely a document of the unconscious fear of the feminine which men, immersed in
a one-sided patriarchy, have over the millennia
projected onto this archetype.

We must visit and come to terms with the dark
unconscious side of our inner nature, for, if we avoid
this realm, we create polarity and eventually develop a dualistic world view. We have to face up to
our inner Hecate, make a relationship with her as
guardian of our unconsciousness, our dark side, and,
trusting her stewardship, allow ourselves to grow
into an awareness of the rich realm of our personal
Underworld. Only through this can we become
integrated beings, able to handle polarities without
immediately projecting the dualisms of 'good' and
'evil' upon events and individuals.

The Bath of Hera on the Ludovisi relief from the Heraeum at Argos

HERA

Hera has a Triple Goddess nature which we can see as complementary to that of Hecate-Artemis. If we look at the mythology of the Hera figure we can see this triplicity quite clearly.

Hera was a daughter of Kronos and Rhea, the great Titan Mother Goddess, and was brought up in Arcadia. The Horae, or three Seasons, were her nurses. Zeus desired her, but Hera resisted the passionate advances of her brother. However, Hera was tricked by devious Zeus, who appeared to her in the form of a cuckoo, cold and frozen by the harshness of winter. Hera, in her role as protectress, felt compassion and warmed this young cuckoo at her breast. Zeus, changing back into his own form, took advantage of their closeness. Hera was forced to submit to his advances, but only yielded to him after extracting a promise of marriage. At her marriage feast, Mother Earth, Gaia, gave Hera as a present the Tree of the Golden Apples of Immortality, which were from that time on guarded by the three Hesperides in Hera's orchard. This shows a further triplicity connected with Hera.

Hera became the celestial Queen of Olympus and was represented as such in many statues, perhaps the most famous being that by Polyclitus in the Heraeum at Argos. This was a colossal statue, in gold and ivory, representing the Goddess on her throne, her crown adorned with figures of the Graces and the Seasons, a pomegranate in one hand and in the other a scepter with a cuckoo on the top. She was often shown with her sacred bird, the peacock.

Hera sets the archetype for woman in relationship to man within a patriarchal social order, as ideal wife and companion. Thus she is a Goddess of marriage (Gamilea), maternity and fidelity, a jealous guardian of the marriage vows and heredity. During the patriarchal period, Hera was elevated to this role as protectress of the ideal wife, but we can see through this the traces of her earlier Triple Goddess form.

The Ludovisi image of Hera

At an earlier time, Hera was the Triple Goddess of the three stages of woman's life. There were three temples dedicated to her at Stymphalus in her forms of Hera-Pais (Child-Goddess), Hera-Thelia (Bride-Goddess), and Hera-Chera (Widow-Goddess). Her triple facets are revealed in her various names. First she was the child Parthenia, the virgin facet of the Goddess, also named Antheia, the 'flowering one.' Next she became Teleia, the 'fulfilled one,' the Mother facet, and was then named Nympheuomene, 'she who seeks a mate.' In her representation of the later stage of woman's life she became Theria, 'old woman or crone,' through which aspect woman was inwardly reborn to her wisdom facet.

Hera's three facets link her to the three Seasons and the three phases of the Moon. In her earliest appearance in myth she is associated with the cow, showing her connection with fecundity and birth, especially associated by the Greeks with this animal. She renewed her virginity each year by bathing in the stream Canathos near Argos, a place especially sacred to her. Thus we see that she bears within herself the archetype of eternal renewal, like the cycling of the Moon herself through her phases. By this act she also links together the cycle of the Moon, the female menstrual cycle, and the cycle of the vegetative year.

We should note especially the polarity that exists between this Hera archetype of woman—the outer facet of a woman's life, the conscious, light-filled,

Ouranian side—and with the Artemis-Hecate facet, which is more concerned with the inner independence, the relationship with the unconscious, the chthonic darkness within our being.

THE JUDGEMENT OF PARIS

This is an important myth in the Greek cycle, as it shows the folly of man when he relates to only one facet of the Triple Goddess, or puts one facet above the others. This myth begins with an impulse of the Goddess Eris ('strife'), who was not invited to the wedding of the mortal Peleus and the sea Goddess Thetis. Eris, true to character, decided to sow some discord, and sent into this banquet of the Gods a golden apple as prize for the fairest and most beautiful Goddess. Hera, Artemis and Aphrodite all claimed the prize and Zeus was called in to arbitrate and judge. He refused, for being a spiritual agency, he was aware that there can be no hierarchy within the Triple Goddess; all three of her facets are complementary, and none stand spiritually above the others. Zeus decided to place this decision into the sphere of humanity, in a sense to test its maturity. One telling of this myth relates that Zeus had at this time grown tired of humanity and wished to place difficulties into the human sphere. Therefore Zeus asked that the choice be made by a man, and Paris, of noble birth, handsome of form, and possessing wisdom, was elected to pass judgement.

Hermes brought the three Goddesses before Paris and asked him to choose which of them was the fairest. Paris was initially wise enough to refuse, saying that as a mortal man he could not make such a choice, and that he would rather divide the apple equally among the three Goddesses. But Hermes insisted, saying that if Paris did not choose one above the others he would incur the wrath of Zeus. Paris still hesitated, worrying about the responsibility, but when the Goddesses agreed to abide by his decision whatever it may be, he acceded to their demand. He asked that the three should disrobe and appear separately before him quite naked.

Hera came first and displayed herself to him, offering as a bribe to make him Lord of Asia and the richest man in the world if he would choose her.

Next came Athene, and she in turn attempted to bribe him with the promise of victory in all his battles and to make him the wisest man in the world.

Aphrodite was last of the three, but she knew her power over man, and in her splendid nakedness began to flirt with him. Paris was, of course, affected by her closeness and advances, and when she promised him by way of a bribe to give him as a mistress Helen of Sparta, a mortal woman as beautiful and passionate as herself, he found it impossible to refuse. He awarded the apple to Aphrodite.

The pride of the other two facets, Hera and Athene, was deeply hurt by this pronouncement, and they decided to plot the downfall of the young man. Thus were set in motion the events which led to the Trojan War.

This myth of the Judgement of Paris is important because it holds in its kernel one of the central problems of the relationship of the human sexes. As we have striven in this book to indicate, the inner archetype of the feminine is threefold; it should be obvious that a one-dimensional relationship to a single facet of the Goddess must lead to inner difficulties and strife. Paris, as representative of humanity, makes his Judgement that the alluring Aphrodite facet of woman is primary. He puts his sexual attraction to woman before any other consideration, downgrading the Athene-wisdom facet or the Hera-Mother aspect. This leads to polarization and a battle between the Trojans and Greeks for possession of the most beautiful woman in the world. Thus we see that a reduction of the archetypal femininity to a single dimension of sexual attraction leads to polarization in the masculine sphere; eventually two rival polarized groups battle against each other for possession of the feminine. We can recognize how the Judgement of Paris marked the beginning impulse of patriarchy and the strife and polarization it brought into social relationships.

Through the Judgement of Paris, which still occurs in our souls today, one facet of the feminine is elevated to a superior position and the other two facets are downgraded. In this way men often deny themselves a true and complete experience of the feminine, and women are forced to work with this one current in the human soul. They are encouraged to be more attracted to developing their Aphrodite facet, often denying and repressing the otherwise complementary sides of their natures. This can lead to great distortions, unfulfilled potential, and personal unhappiness, both for women and men in our society. We should not see the Judgement of Paris as merely an interesting Greek myth, but rather as an ongoing event in the souls of men and women today. Because artists are sensitive to and reflect the archetypes within their souls and the soul of humanity, it is not surprising that the Judgement of Paris was one of the most popular themes in Renaissance painting.

Additional Examples of
the Triple Goddess
Found in Various Traditions

THE THRIAE

The Thriae were a triad of Goddesses forming a
Triple Muse of Divination at Delphi. They taught
Hermes how to foretell the future by gazing at the
dance of pebbles in a vessel of water. They were
Goddesses connected with the earliest period of the
Delphic Oracle, when it was presided over by a
female Pythia or priestess of divination. This occurred long before the sacred center was won over to
patriarchal control and re-dedicated to Apollo. They
were connected with a mystery center called the
Corycian Cave high on the shoulder of Mount Parnassus; this is now thought to be the site of the early
matriarchal period of the Delphic Oracle, which was
moved to its better known site at Delphi, at the foot
of Mount Parnassus, sometime in the eighth century B.C. The Three Sisters were named Korykia,
Daphnis, and Thuia in certain stories. As manifestations of the Triple Goddess, they practiced a mantic
art of foretelling the future through entering into
some kind of dream-like state. They were especially
connected with the bee and required offerings of
honey before they would undertake divination.

THE AUGRALIDS

The Augralids were an ancient triplet of Earth
Goddesses worshipped by the pre-Hellenic peoples
of Attica. They ruled the area around Athens long
before the Greek Athene came to prominence. There
is an interesting set of stories that record in mythic

terms the passing of spiritual power from this ancient Triple Goddess to the rising Athene. The Augralids, three sisters, were the daughters of Cecrops. They were called Agraulos, Herse and Pandrosos, and their names show them to be deities of the fertilizing dew. They were entrusted by Athene with a box they were told to guard but not to open. Of course, their curiosity eventually overcame their better judgement, and, opening the box just for a peek at what it contained, released a terrible snake called Erichthonious ('the earth born'). This led to their downfall. In some stories they met their death. In others they were made to be entirely in the service of Athene, and to give fruitfulness to the fields. They were forced to surrender any power they might have had over the destinies of people and became only Goddesses of the Earth.

AL-LAT, AL-UZZA AND MENAT

Long before the coming of the austere patriarchal system of Islam, the Arabic people worshipped this trinity of desert Goddesses who were the three facets of the one Goddess. Al-Uzza ('the mighty') represented the Virgin warrior facet; she was a desert Goddess of the morning star who had a sanctuary in a grove of acacia trees to the south of Mecca, where she was worshipped in the form of a sacred stone. Al-Lat, whose name simply means 'Goddess,' was the Mother facet connected with the Earth and its fruits, and ruler of fecundity. She was worshipped at At Ta'if near Mecca in the form of a great uncut block of white granite. Menat, the crone facet of the Goddess, ruled fate and death. Her principal sanctuary was located on the road between Mecca and Medina, where she was worshipped in the form of a black uncut stone. Mohammed, in his struggle to establish his male dominated religion, persecuted the worshippers of the Goddess and destroyed her shrines. Interestingly, it seems that Mohammed, having found it difficult to overcome the worship of the sacred stones of the Goddess, instead replaced this ritual custom with one within his religion, as the Christian church in Europe had done with discomforting ancient pagan customs. Thus he instituted the worship of the great Holy Stone of Islam, the Kaaba in Mecca.

GOLLVEIG, HEIDER AND ANGERBODA

Norse mythology was written down very late, long after the masculine element had dominated its myths; consequently it is difficult to find many clear examples of the Triple Goddess. However, I believe we have in the figures of Gollveig, Heider and Angerboda a record of the Triple Goddess from an early stratum of Norse myth. The Voluspa Saga tells of the first war of all time. It was caused by a rivalry between the Aesir and Vanir hierarchies of Gods. At the start of this conflict Gollveig, presumably a relation of the Vanir, was pierced with spears and burnt to death in the hall of the High One (Odin). She was three times burnt and three times reborn, and was also called Heider, a far seeing witch cunning in sorcery. It has been suggested that her third rebirth was as Angerboda, a wife of Loki. Loki fathered upon Angerboda three terrible beings of fate and destiny. The first of these beings was the Fenris Wolf who would eventually swallow the world at the time of Ragnarok. The second was the Midgard Serpent, who gnawed at the roots of the Tree of Life. Last, in this trinity of spiritual agencies connected with the destiny of the worlds, is Hel, the Queen of the nine layers of the Underworld, called Nifelheim. This myth seems to lead us back to an earlier stratum of Goddesses, although due to a patriarchal point of view they were depicted as giving rise to terrible negative forces working in destiny. Unlike Greek mythology, much of the positive side of the feminine component of the spiritual worlds has been lost to Norse mythology. However, one surely cannot doubt that at an earlier time there were profound tales told of the positive aspects of the Goddess, now lost in the written tradition.

THE VALKYRIES

The Valkyries are the 'Choosers of the Slain' in Norse mythology and correspond to some extent to the Greek Erinyes. However, they do not seem to possess the Greek vengeance for matricide, the protection of the female blood-line, that is bound up with the Erinyes. Norse mythology was written down during an extremely patriarchal warrior stage in the development of Germanic-Scandinavian societies, and thus the Valkyries, though doubtless remnants of an earlier Triple Goddess, are intimately connected with the heroic masculine. They are the choosers of the slain, and bring those noble souls who have lost their lives in battle into the company of Odin, where they have their eternal reward. However, the names of the Valkyries, as preserved in some stories, retain a conception of the wild primal energies of the Erinyes; consider the names Hlokk ('the Shrieking One'), Goll ('the Screamer') and Skogul ('the Raging One').

The Valkyries are rarely pictured as three in number, but they almost invariably appear in multiples of three, as the Nine, or the Three Nines, and even as the Nine Nines in one story. The Valkyries were such a powerful archetype to the Norse soul that in later times they were seen to have a soft and gentle facet to their nature and could appear as Swan Maidens. The Norse wished so much to soften and mollify the terrible primal facet of the Goddess that they represented her in a gentler form, and thus the Valkyries could at times assume the form of the gentle Swan Maidens. We noted in an earlier section how this softening of the harshness of the primal Goddess occurred in Greek tradition when the Erinyes were transformed into the Eumenides.

THE MOTHERS IN *FAUST*

In the Second Part of Goethe's *Faust*, there is a scene in which Faust stands before the Emperor and promises him a show of Magic that will raise the spirits of Paris and Helen of Troy and present them before the court. Mephistopheles is dismayed, saying that such a thing is outside his power. To accomplish this feat, Faust must first descend into the realm of the Mothers—primal chthonic Goddesses in the depths of the Earth—a realm "That Earth disclaims and Hell is loath to name." Goethe here suggests a Triple Goddess of the chthonic depths, who existed before the polarities of Earth and Hell were established, and are thus more powerful than Mephistopheles. Faust sinks down into the Earth with a luminous key that can unlock the door to their realm, and encounters these shadowy forms gathered around a Golden Tripod, "Goddesses throned in solitude sublime,/Set in no place, still less in any time."

THE NORNS

In Norse mythology the Three Norns represented the Triple Goddess of Fate. They were named in the legends as Urd (the Past), Verdandi (the Present) and Skuld (the Future). They were three spinners who sat at the Well of Urd, situated at one of the roots of the

World Tree Yggdrasil, and they dispensed their fate upon Gods and humankind alike. The Norns belong to the earliest stratum of Norse Mythology, coming from a more primal age than that of Odin or the Aesir and Vanir groups of Gods. They sprinkle water from their well on the roots of the World Tree tingeing it white; indeed, the waters of Urd turn all things white. By eternally renewing their whiteness, these three sisters have been identified as a Triple Moon Goddess with Urd (the waxing crescent Moon), Verdandi (the full Moon disc) and Skuld (the waning Moon).

The English name of these Fates was Wyrd (from Urd). Under the name of the Weird Sisters ('weird' in the sense of 'fate') they entered into English literature and folk legend and story. We have noted them especially in Shakespeare's *Macbeth*, in turn based on Holinshed's *Chronicles.*

THE RHINEMAIDENS

Wagner's great Ring Cycle, based upon the ancient Germanic legend of the *Nibelungenlied*, opens with three Rhinemaidens guarding their treasure of gold at the bottom of the Rhine. This gold had a magic transformative power over all who came to possess it, and the whole drama of the Ring turns on the ways in which it transforms the characters. The magic gold is, at the beginning of the tale, guarded by the Triple Goddess pictured as the Rhinemaidens. In the opening act the Dwarf Albrecht comes to their sacred place, is charmed by a vision of their gold, and learns its secret. To possess it he must renounce the inner power of love in his soul. He does so and forges a ring of power from the Rhinegold. All who subsequently come into the aura of this golden ring are polarized and transformed; egotism and lust after independent power and domination leads to the

Alberich with the Rhinemaidens. Illustration by Arthur Rackham.

downfall of many of the characters in the drama, and creates the final denouement in the Gotterdammerung. Wagner, through this myth of the Nibelungen, points out that the guardianship of this self-destructive spiritual gold lies in the hands of the primal Triple Goddess. Humanity is safe while the Rhinemaidens guard their hoard at the bottom of the Rhine. When it falls into masculine hands, such as those of Albrecht, Woden, Fafnir and Fasholt, or Loki, polarization and dissent result from its spell. In a sense this myth speaks of the dangers of the spiritual forces in the soul working one-sidedly through one facet of humanity, the masculine, which so readily falls into dualism, with its fruits of conflict and bloody struggle.

THE TRIPLE GODDESS IN SHAKESPEARE

The power and perception inherent in Shakespeare's plays arises from his sensitivity to the archetypes working in the psyche. Many of his plays are, in fact, the working out in dramatic form of transformative processes between the archetypes he perceived. It is the universal and archetypal nature of his characters which has preserved the plays and makes them speak to the human condition even some four centuries after they were written. Shakespeare's plays often revolve around the relationship of the masculine and feminine, so it is not surprising that he introduces the Triple Goddess as an important aspect in some of them.

The most obvious example of this must be the Three Witches in *Macbeth*, who meet at one point with Hecate. In the first act of the play we see these three intoning their spell together before meeting with Macbeth and telling him his fate:

The Weird Sisters, hand in hand,
Posters of the sea and land,
Thus go about, about;
Thrice to thine, and thrice to mine,
And thrice again to make up nine,
Peace! the charm's wound up.

The
Weird
Sisters

    Another example can be seen in King Lear, in which the aged King, having no male offspring, decides at the beginning of the play to divide his kingdom equally among his three daughters, Goneril, Regan and Cordelia. The power and dramatic tension of the play derive from the way in which he relates to these three daughters. By denying Cordelia, who refuses to flatter him with empty protestations of love, he divides the kingdom equally between the other two sisters, thus breaking the inner balance of the triplicity and bringing the evils of dualism into his land. Goneril and Regan become hard and deceitful, creating antipathy and opposition which manifests itself in a dreadful war and terrible deeds. This outer disharmony is mirrored in Lear's inner struggle and his descent into madness;

however, Shakespeare intends us to see this as a transformative process in the soul of Lear, an inner transmutation and redemption. He based his tragedy of Lear upon the ancient British legend of King Ludd of Lyr, recounted in Geoffrey of Monmouth's *History*. It may be that this legend of Lyr and his daughters is a picture, in mythic terms, of the struggle between the Threefold Goddess and the patriarchal order.

ERIU, BANBA AND FOTLA

In the Irish "Book of Invasions" which charts, in mythological terms, the various families of divinities that held sway in Ireland over the millennia, there is an interesting tale told of the coming of the Milesians—perhaps the first human inhabitants— to Ireland. They arrive on the shores of Ireland and find it already occupied by the Gods and Goddesses of the land, the Tuatha de Danaan (the children of Dana-Anu). After a magical battle, the Tuatha de Danaan realize that their tenure of the land is now over, their cycle is ending, and that they should relinquish power to the newcomers. They retreat into their Brochs, Cairns or Sidhe, entering into the Earth, the very land itself. On their way inland to the central stronghold of the Danaans, the Milesians, under their leader Amergin, meet with three Goddesses, protectors of the land of Ireland. They are Eriu, Banba and Fotla. These three greet Amergin and make certain prophecies regarding the Milesians' relationship to the land. They ask that the land should be named after them in perpetuity. Only one of these names, that of Eriu, has survived; in the name Eire we thus find preserved a memory of this ancient primal Triple Goddess handing over power to the masculine forces of the invading Milesians. The Milesians' cycle of legends is particularly dominated by the heroic cycle, and, from this point on, Celtic mythology becomes tipped more towards the masculine and emphasizes the deeds of heroes and the clash of arms. The earlier Cycle of the Tuatha de Danaan, to which Eriu, Banba and Fotla belong, is more balanced and obviously comes from a time when the Celtic peoples were more open to the balancing of the masculine and feminine elements in their souls and consequently reflected this in their mythology.

BRIGIT, BRIGHID OR BRIDE

Brighid is one of the major Triple Goddesses of the Irish Celts and is especially important in the Scottish tradition. She had three distinct facets, being seen as Goddess of Smithcraft, of Healing, and of Poetry.

She was especially connected with the element of fire, and her three facets can be seen as fire operating on different levels of being. Thus, as Brighid the Smith-Goddess, she aided those who worked outwardly with fire to fashion metals, the craftsmen and smiths. As Brighid the Healer, she nourished the inner fire of life and aided those who worked as healers of the sick, trying to give back to those who were diseased their inner fire of life, their etheric life force. As Brighid the Poet-Goddess, she brought the fire of inspiration into the souls of those who worked to create poetry and music. So we can see that Brighid sustained the Fire that transforms us on the material, etheric and astral levels of our beings.

In ancient times, Brigit was venerated at her mystery center at Kildare in Ireland, which was under the guardianship of nine priestesses (befitting a Triple Goddess). Brigit was such an important Goddess in the Irish tradition that after the Christianization of Ireland the Church saw little point in

Romano-British statue of Brigantia, or Brighid, found in southwest Scotland

trying to destroy her worship, so deeply was her veneration instilled into the soul of the people. Instead she was 'Christianized' into St. Brigit, and to this day remains one of the most loved Saints in Ireland. In some stories it was St. Patrick himself who baptized her into Christianity, and she was elevated to the status of a Gaelic Mary figure, often being seen as the midwife to Mary and even the wet-nurse of the Christ child. After her Christianization her mystery center at Kildare was turned into a shrine and a sisterhood of nuns was formed to care and tend this sacred place. It is said that nineteen nuns tended this shrine, keeping a flame perpetually alight on her altar. They would take this task upon themselves in turn for nineteen nights, but on the twentieth, it was said that the spirit of St. Brigit miraculously kept the flame alight.

Brighid was at an early time also seen as a Goddess connected with the yearly cycle. She presided over the beginning of Spring which, in the cycle of the ancient fire festivals—Samhain, Imbolc, Beltane, and Lammas—was on the eve of the first of February, Imbolc, or Brighid's Day (later to be Christianized as Candlemas). Through the cycle of the Fire Festivals ancient Celtic peoples celebrated the different energies in the turning of the wheel of the year. This was experienced especially as the power of fire manifesting on different levels. Thus they worked fire rituals to encourage and empathize with the inner fire of the Earth which ebbed and flowed like a tide through the seasons. The time of Brighid's Eve was set aside for the celebration of the Fire of Illumination; the impulses of inspiration, of healing, and of creative energy were experienced on that night as the dark of winter began to give way to the coming forces of Spring.

This picture was especially preserved in the Scottish legends of Brighid's relationship to the Cailleach. The Cailleach, also known as the Carline or Mag-

Moullach, was the hag aspect of the Goddess in the yearly cycle. She was connected with the dark and cold of Winter and took up her rule in the cycle of the seasons at Samhain, the eve of the first of November. She bore the black rod of Winter and smote the land with cold contractive forces that withered the vegetation. As the end of Winter approached she gave over her rod of power to Brighid, in whose hands it became a white rod that stimulated the germination of the seeds lying buried in the dark earth. The expansive forces of nature would then begin to unfold. Sometimes these two Goddesses were pictured as battling for control of the nature forces: the Cailleach even was said to imprison Brighid under the mountains in Winter. However, we can better see them as two facets of a Triple Goddess of the Seasons: the Hag-Cailleach of Winter, the Maiden-Brighid of Spring, and a Mother Goddess of Summer's lushness and Autumn's fruiting. The name of the last member of this triplicity has not been so carefully preserved in folk legend. Perhaps this is because she represented a facet of the Goddess which was too pagan, too connected with fecundity and the sexual forces of life, for the Church to allow her to be openly worshipped. However, we can recognize some of her attributes in Tailtu, an Irish Earth Mother Goddess associated with Lammas, and in Anu-Dana (sometimes called 'Annie' in folk tradition), the primal Mother Goddess of the Irish Celts. Since the celebration of Brighid's festival involved the fashioning of a Bride Doll from the last corn sheaves of the previous year, we can see that one of her attributes was as a Corn Goddess. In one sense the Cailleach-Brighid figure can be seen to have a parallel with the Demeter-Persephone myth of the ancient Greeks.

The
Deae
Matrones

DEAE MATRONES

The Deae Matrones were a Celtic trinity of Earth
Goddesses whose cult was celebrated during the
times of the Roman occupation of the Celtic regions
of Gaul and Britain. Their existence was recorded by
Roman historians. Quite a few sculptures remain
depicting these three fertility Goddesses, who are
most often shown as three robed women bearing
baskets or cornucopias of fruit or flowers, and are
sometimes shown holding children in their arms.
Usually only the central figure is shown standing.
Very little is known of these Goddesses except that
they seem to be a Triple Mother Goddess connected
with the fecundity of humankind and the fertility of
the land. It has been suggested that one of these
statues preserved from Druidical times stood in an
underground sanctuary on the site where Chartres
cathedral was later built. This statue was venerated

as the famous 'Black Virgin' of Chartres, to which many people made pilgrimage in medieval times.

THE THREE MARIES

Christianity can hardly be said to be a religion of the Goddess, but from about the 12th century onward the cult of the Virgin Mary was established and emphasized in the Catholic Church. The figure of Mary as simultaneously Virgin and Mother of necessity gave rise to some inner difficulties and contradictions for the worshippers, but in time a new archetype of ideal womanhood was fashioned by the Catholic Church around this figure. This Mary figure is pure and perfect, standing above sin; indeed she did not die bodily because her flesh was so perfect that she was transported into heaven as a physical being, as recounted in the relatively late doctrine of the Assumption of the Virgin. As she is an impossible archetype for women to live up to, this Mary figure is really a projection of men's view, and in particular a celibate male priesthood's view, of what is spiritually archetypal in woman.

Although the present Mary archetype is less useful in our age, we can look back to its importance during the beginnings of Christianity. During the first few centuries after the events surrounding its founder, we see a religious movement that was more open to the feminine than the patriarchal Judaism in which Jesus was brought up and against which he reacted with his new insight into the nature of divinity. Early Christianity was open to the feminine and incorporated it into its mythology in the gospels, even though the Apostle Paul was not happy with any focus on the feminine. Thus we note the Three Maries who appear at the tomb of the resurrection are an important part of early Christian iconography. These are Mary the Virgin, Mary wife of

Cleopas, and Mary Magdelene, and in a minor way perhaps have introduced an element of the Triple Goddess into patriarchal Christianity, though the spiritual or esoteric significance of these Three Maries was not further developed in orthodox Christianity. They did, however, play a part in certain Gnostic schools.

THE MORRIGAN

The Morrigan is the terrible hag Goddess of Irish legend. She bears some relationship to the Furies or Erinyes and even to the Valkyries of Norse myth. She appears as a Triple Goddess of Battle and depicts the harsh unrelenting warrior side of the Celtic soul. Her three facets were named individually as 'the Morrigan,' the 'phantom Queen' or 'queen of nightmares'; Badb, the 'Crow' or 'Raven'; and Macha, who personified 'frenzy' and the heat of battle.

THE THREE VIRTUES

Following Roman tradition, the Christian theological virtues, Faith, Hope and Charity (or Love), were often portrayed as three Goddesses.

LILITH, 'ISHAH AND EVE: THREE GODDESSES IN THE GARDEN

Perhaps the myth most formative in structuring the psyche of Western humanity is that of the Fall of Man through woman in the Garden of Eden. This *Genesis* picture has provided Western Christianity with an awful dualism; it gives us a picture of a state of Edenic spiritual perfection, from the joys of which we have fallen through our sexual nature, via the temptation of Eve. The patriarchs of Judaism so greatly feared the power of the feminine that they wove this myth which has brought so much misery to humankind. By tainting the relationship of the sexes as unspiritual and 'earthly' in opposition to a supposed 'heavenly' spirituality, and by particularly picturing this as having occurred through the wiles of the woman facet, they blamed the figure of Eve for the 'Fall.' The consequence of this has been the casting out of women from any significant participation in the spiritual life of Western humanity. Indeed, many women have, over the millennia, been ruthlessly persecuted for intruding upon this cherished male preserve. However, if we look at the legend of the Garden found in other sources than the Bible, particularly in esoteric kabbalistic commentaries upon the Creation, some Goddesses seem to be lurking in the background.

We can see a triplicity of female partners of Adam, the Archetypal Man. Adam's first wife, Lilith, made like him from the dust of the Earth, is shown in the patriarchal legends of the Talmud as being an evil figure who sought equality with Adam. In fact, she saw herself as his equal and wanted a full share in the pleasures of lovemaking. As a female principle, no doubt the remnant of an ancient Goddess tradition of pre-patriarchal times, Lilith was antipathetic to the later patriarchal values. She was therefore inverted and turned into a figure of evil. She was especially associated with the snake, like many other Goddesses of the hag facet. The snake or dragon actually symbolizes living forces of the Earth and the active energies of the feminine; it was thus seen to be in conflict with the active creative energies of the masculine.

In Judaism, Jehovah, known as the Moon God, usurped the creative role of the Moon Goddess. In later times Lilith, originally an equal partner with Adam, became instead the patroness of evil incubi

A Sumerian representation of Lilith

and succubi; she was the promoter of erotic dreams and nightmares, the destroyer of little children. At this point Eve emerged as a female principle more in harmony with patriarchal values: she is made from the rib of Adam. As an emanation of his power, she is his helpmate and subservient companion. Not only is she made to shoulder the responsibility for humanity's trespass against the Father God's absurd ordinance, but the patriarchs were thus able to blame womankind, through the Eve myth, for the evil and dualism they perceived in themselves and the universe. Their own dualism caused an inability to attain an ideal spirituality; it was unattainable, in fact, because it denied their earthly nature.

The myth of the Fall was brought in rather late in the Jewish tradition, and the creation story in *Genesis* was in fact formed by uniting two separate versions. These versions reveal another facet of the Goddess in the Garden in the form of 'Ishah. Adam, the archetypal man, called 'Ish in one of these stories, and 'Ishah, are two parts of one being, an hermaphroditic archetype of humanity, two emanations of masculine and feminine attributes in incarnation. Thus we have in fact a triplicity of Goddesses in the Garden, Lilith, 'Ishah and Eve. Lilith and Eve are two extreme polarities of the archetypal feminine created of the dualistic consciousness of the patriarchal Judaic priesthood. Lilith, the dark evil one, is sometimes pictured as the serpent, even as the wife of Satan. Eve, the fallen archetype of woman who, through her own imperfection, brought ruin upon humanity and must eternally suffer, is inferior to the masculine principle she compromised. 'Ishah appears in the creation story as a shadowy reflection of a third facet of the Goddess in harmony with the masculine, her name reflecting that of 'Ish, the archetypal male.

CHINNAMASTA

Chinnamasta is one of the ten facets of the Indian Goddess Kali. These facets or transformations of Kali are sometimes called Mahavidyas. Meditation upon them is an essential part of Tantric esotericism.

At first appearance Chinnamasta is a gruesome sight, garlanded with snakes, with blood spurting from her severed head; however, if she is perceived as a symbolic figure for meditation and not naively

Chinnamasta

as a terrible ghoul, much can be gained from the power of the archetypes bound up in her form.

She is always shown standing or seated upon two lovers in sexual union. These are usually Krishna and Radha, representing Vishnu and Lakshmi, the two emanations of the divine principle as the male and female forces in nature and the human realm. Our experience of the Chinnamasta aspect of our souls can only begin when we have begun to unite the male and female polarities of our being. If we work with Tantric yoga, we shall eventually be given an inner vision of Chinnamasta standing upon our lower sexual chakra or center. There are three streams in the soul: the Ida (lunar), Pingala (solar), and the central Sushumna, which interweaves these two in a balanced form. It is the transformation of these three streams that the Chinnamasta figure brings before us. Just as the male and female facets of our souls cannot flow into each other until they have abandoned their defenses and open up to each other in the lower soul, so in our upper soul, our 'head aspect,' the same dualities cannot be bridged until the head is similarly opened up. That is why the rather gruesome picture of Chinnamasta's severed head appears. What is really pictured in this image (see previous page) is the opening of the upper soul. To prevent it from falling into duality, we see Chinnamasta's own head receiving the essence of the blood only from the united Sushumna channel, while the polarized energies of the Ida and Pingala streams are instead taken up by her two servant figures Dakini and Barnini.

These streams can also be associated with the Three Gunas: Tamas, the dark, inert, feminine; Sattva, the radiant, expansive, masculine; and Rajas, the balancing. Tamas and Sattva comprise the left and right channels, respectively; Rajas represents the interweaving Mercury from the well of the soul. The Chinnamasta picture shows that unless we balance the energies of masculine and feminine in our lower souls, our upper head consciousness will itself be unbalanced. If it tends to Sattva-Pingala there will be too much objectivity and detachment. If the left channel is too active and one tends too much toward Tamas, formless, aimless desire within one's consciousness, flitting from one thought to another, will result.

This horrific and terrible Triple Goddess figure, in fact, contains a profound wisdom of the inner functioning of our psyches.

SHAKTI

It is well known that the Hindu religion has at its center a triplicity of Gods—Brahma (the Creator), Siva (the Transformer) and Vishnu (the Preserver). Each of these three Gods has as consort a female companion called a Shakti. At one time early in Indian traditions, such consorts were seen merely as emanations of the individual male Gods; however, from about the fifth century A.D. onwards, the Goddess began to become an important archetype for the Indian consciousness. During this period the Shaktis became very important deities and were worshipped in their own right. In time they adopted qualities and characteristics associated with a more primal level of Goddess worship going back many millennia in the Eastern traditions.

Brahma had Sarasvati as his consort. She embodied nature and was the patroness of the arts and crafts, and she especially reflected the Mother facet of the Triple Goddess. Siva, the transformer or destroyer God, had Kali as his special companion. She represented the black hag aspect of the Triple Goddess and was the initiatrix into transcendence. Siva also united with Parvati who, in a sense, can be seen as the light side of Kali. Vishnu, the final member of this trinity and the preserver of order and stability in the world, had Lakshmi as his Shakti. She was portrayed as young and very beautiful and is the ideal faithful wife as well as the Maiden facet of the Goddess.

The Eastern traditions have many examples of the Triple Goddess. A full description of these would require a full scale study to do it justice. This is particularly true of the ideas of tantric esotericism which deal with the balancing of masculine and feminine polarities in the soul.

In the Indian tradition, the active feminine side of creation worked through three aspects. These are rather abstract metaphysical concepts and did not make for popular Goddesses with whom the common people could readily identify. However, we can see the Triple Goddess archetype in the triplicity of Maya, Shakti, and Prakriti. Maya is the web of the universe. She eternally performs her dance of illusion, making the world seemingly substantial, solid and materially tangible. Those who know her better realize that all such solidity is an illusion, a nonmaterial spiritual force woven into seeming substantiality. Shakti, on the other hand, is pure spiritual energy manifesting in a feminine form. According to tradition, the masculine facet of the spiritual gave form, but had no inner energy until united with Shakti. Shakti is the living energy woven by her sister Maya. Meanwhile, Prakriti is the cosmic root substance, the essence or archetype of the material. She is immanent, eternally potential, in the emptiness of space. She is present everywhere but does not manifest herself outwardly. She is depicted as the grains or focal points in the void around which raw spiritual energy swirls and flows, producing the semblance of atoms and solid substance. Maya takes her archetype of substance together with the energy of Shakti into her dance and weaves before our consciousness the illusory forms and substance of the material world.

The Graces
of Botticelli's
"Primavera"

THE GRACES OF BOTTICELLI'S "PRIMAVERA"

Sandro Botticelli's "Primavera," which is recognized as one of the most beautiful paintings in Western art, is also a subtle document of Renaissance Neoplatonism. The painting was executed under the patronage of Lorenzo di Pierfrancesco, a pupil of the Florentine Neoplatonist Ficino. Botticelli's painting shows the relationship between earthly and spiritual love, and in particular depicts the three Graces engaged in an elaborate dance. In Neoplatonic terms these Three Graces differ somewhat from the Greek conception of the Charities. Rather they are the trinity of Voluptas, Castitas and Pulchritudo; or, otherwise, Laetitia Uberima, Viriditas and Splendor. The Graces dance in a group. The one in the foreground with her back towards the viewer is Castitas or Viriditas, the youthful innocent Grace, entering upon the path of love. To the left of her is Voluptas, the facet of the Triplicity that enjoys the earthly pleasures of love. To the right is Pulchritudo, whose outer beauty and fairness of form and her dreamy, slightly detached gaze indicate her inner dwelling upon the spiritual facet of love. This is expressed in her fairness of form and her adornments. The innocent Virgin facet of the Three Graces mediates between these two aspects of love, and the interweaving of the hands of these dancers in Venus' garden shows that there is little danger of this trinity of Goddesses falling into the trap of dualism. In these Graces of Botticelli the earthly and the spiritual are eternally and quintessentially intertwined.

SUGGESTIONS AND HINTS
FOR FURTHER RESEARCH

I have chosen to focus this book on the Triple
Goddess as seen in Greek mythology because this
field is so rich in Goddess material. Greek thought
was so pure in the classical period that the forms of
the myths have been well preserved. This allows us
to see the inner architecture of the Triple Goddess
archetype and the ways in which she was fashioned
and changed as Greek society changed and became
more patriarchal.

It would be quite wrong, however, for the reader to
remain with the impression that the Triple Goddess
is primarily connected with Greek mythology and
religion, so I have included in this additional section
some summarized descriptions of examples from
other traditions. There is, in fact, a mass of material
on the Triple Goddess archetype. One often must
search hard for it, however, as most of the male
academic writers of past centuries were not especially intrigued by the feminine in mythology and
tended to concentrate upon hero myths. There is,
additionally, a very broad spectrum of material on
the Universal Goddess contained in all the spiritual
traditions and mythologies of the world. There has
not been space within the small compass of this
book to itemize all of these examples of the archetype, and I have had to leave out of consideration a
great deal of interesting and valuable material. In
addition, I am certainly not expert in many fields of
mythology; there must be many fascinating examples to be found in traditions which I am not
acquainted with.

To conclude this section, I would just like to point

to some further avenues for research for those who wish to explore the archetype further. Looking at mythological and legendary material through the archetype of the Triple Goddess will give one much insight into the inner relationships and structure of such mythic material.

ARTHURIAN LEGEND: In Arthurian legend there are three female figures who are important in shaping Arthur's direction and destiny. These are his sister Morgan le Fay, his wife Guinevere, and his spiritual protectress, the Lady of the Lake, who gave him his magical sword. These can be seen as facets of the Triple Goddess. At the death of Arthur, the three Queens who bear him away in a barge to the Island of Avalon are the Queen Morgan le Fay, the Queen of Northgales and the Queen of the Wastelands.

MABINOGION: In the Celtic legends of the Welsh tradition, there are a number of Goddesses who can be seen as forming triplicities. For example, there is the triad of Arionrhod, Rhiannon and Blodeuwed. Our main sources for this Welsh material are manuscripts of the thirteenth and fourteenth centuries, in which these myths have been written down in a euhemerized form; that is, the Gods and Goddesses of an earlier mythological stratum were turned into human figures with spiritual powers. It is difficult to untangle the threads of earlier layers of myth especially when they have been interwoven with hero tales from other traditions to make up such documents as the *Mabinogion*. Perhaps some insights into this material can be gained by exploring the Goddess forms within it.

THE BOOK OF REVELATION: There are three symbolic figures in the *Book of Revelation* that can be associated with the facets of the Triple Goddess:

the Harlot, or Whore of Babylon, obviously the hag aspect; the Woman clothed with the Sun with the Moon at her feet, the Mother facet; and the Bride of the Christ, the personification of the City of the New Jerusalem.

THE CABIRIAN NYMPHS: One of the most important of the Greek chthonic mystery centers was on the island of Samothrace. It was there that the mysteries of Cabiri were celebrated. Initiates were given an inner experience of the spiritual potentialities woven into the earthly material world, the inner fire in matter. During the later period three Gods seem to have been celebrated there. They were Axieros, Axiocersa, and Axiocersus (sometimes also called Casmilus). At an earlier period three Cabirian Nymphs were an important aspect of the mystery. These three were the daughters of Sydic by Hephaistos, who, as the smith-God of the Greeks, was especially connected with these mysteries.

JEWISH ESOTERICISM: The Jewish religious tradition is extremely patriarchal and focused on the Jehovah figure. However, in Jewish esotericism the feminine could not be so absolutely repressed, and several shadowy feminine figures appear as hidden Goddesses behind the outer masculine emanations of the Divine. The Tetragrammaton had as its reflection the Shekinah. The Tetragrammaton, JHVH, was the Four Lettered Name of God. The first letter, JOD, corresponded to the Father; HE, the second letter, represented Shekinah, the Mother facet that proceeded from the Father; VAU was the Son, Messiah or King aspect; and finally, HE, the last letter, corresponded to another feminine emanation, the Matronit, Maiden or Daughter.

The other female figure in the Jewish esoteric tradition was Lilith, associated with the 'evil' Qlipoth. It was believed that if the Matronit and the King were to become separated from each other the Israelites would fall into sin. After separating from Matronit, the King would mate with Lilith. Simultaneously the Prince of Demons, Samael, would seduce the Matronit. Thus we have a triplicity of Shekinah, Matronit and Lilith. The Matronit had to keep herself virginal, for, if she united with Samael, the soul of the Israelites would fall into sin. Another triple element in Jewish Kabbalah are the Three Mother Letters, Aleph, Mem and Shin, each formed by three strokes of the stylus. They are associated with the elements of Air, Water and Fire.

EGYPTIAN GOD FORMS: The Egyptian pantheon is extremely complicated, as the Egyptians were only too ready to project facets of themselves onto external God forms, especially those associated with animal archetypes. At the center of this complex mass of symbolism is the figure of Isis, who as Sister, Wife and Widow of Osiris was a Triple Goddess. However, her three facets are usually totally integrated in her being and she is not seen as splitting into triple aspects, as we have often noted above with the Greek Goddesses. The Triple Goddess archetype may throw light upon some elements of this seeming chaos of Gods and Goddesses, although this would require a great deal of original research and contemplation of the essence of the Egyptian traditions.

THE GNOSTICS: Gnostic documents such as the *Pistis Sophia* display an elevated spiritual perspective. The Gnostic mystery schools came into prominence during the 3rd to 6th centuries A.D. At the same time the Christian Church, having wedded itself to Roman imperialism, was consolidating its ideas within a patriarchal framework. It drew up dogmas, and codified its earlier spiritual insight into frozen forms of ideas and rituals. The Gnostics arose as an antithesis to this development, and their schools were places of instruction in methods of speculation, in the sense of 'seeing into the spiritual world.' Fragments of Gnostic texts that remain show a concern with the feminine, and especially with Sophia, the wisdom aspect of the feminine. It would likely be of value to look at Gnostic thought and speculative images in the light of the archetype of the Triple Goddess.

CONCLUSION

Having presented the reader with this survey or overview of the Triple Goddess archetype and her manifestation in various mythologies, perhaps I should attempt to give some indication as to how one can relate to and use these ideas and archetypes.

Mere intellectual study of mythology is not enough. This has its own dangers anyway of pedanticism and specialization. Within a short time of committing themselves whole-heartedly to a merely intellectual view, students will find themselves buried in a mass of different sources, alternative readings, contradictory versions, and will inevitably lose an overview, an ability to stand outside the material. Mythology once committed to paper and pursued as an academic study loses much of its inner life. Rather, mythology has to be eternally relived in the soul and cannot be engulfed, encompassed, and explained even by the bright fire of an active intellect. Study must only be seen as a beginning, for it will not lead us into the heart of the mystery, but rather leave us picking away at the detailed fringes of alternative versions and having to make judgements as to the validity of sources.

If, as I suggest in this survey, mythology truly lives as archetypes within our souls, we have to go down and meet it, rather than expecting to bring its substance up into our intellectual sphere. What the intellect sees when it relates to these archetypes is more a reflection of the intellect itself than a full experience of the formative impulse of myth. I would therefore like to suggest that we have to try to find other ways of working with the spiritual energies bound up in mythology.

The word 'archetype' has been used extensively in this book, and I feel sure I must owe the reader an explanation of this term. The word itself derives from the Greek *archein*, to begin, and *tupos*, a model, though this gives us but little insight. The word 'archetypal' was used in the Platonic stream and enters into Renaissance Hermeticism. There it is used with the sense of a noumenal Platonic world of Forms, standing above and outside the world of incarnation in which we physically live. This archetypal world contains the essence, the spiritual exo-skeleton of all that is in physical incarnation. Thus we can picture, say, an individual plant having its archetype in this spiritual world of Forms, which like an exo-skeleton gives form, an unchanging and eternal shape, to its various material embodiments on Earth. The individual plant seeks to grow to reflect the archetype, which on one level of its being it perceives as a kind of perfect form or aspiration that it strives toward. This Platonic idea of archetypes as standing far above the material is not that which I have used in this book. Indeed, in a sense this view gives us a 'patriarchal' sky-god picture of the relation between the spiritual and the earthly.

The particular sense of the word 'archetype' used here derives from the work of C.G. Jung, though interpreted in a more esoteric manner. To Jung, an archetype represented a structure in the unconscious part of the human psyche. It belonged not so much to the individual as to the particular race and tradition within which this individual was born and brought up. The archetypes are, in this sense, the remnants of experiences of our ancestors and, collectively, of the race to which we belong. A hard line behaviorist would be tempted to describe these as part of a racially inherited programming of the brain.

Esotericists and spiritual philosophers of our present age recognized in Jung's picture of the human psyche some facets that resonated with their own conception and experience of the soul forces. They especially found that his idea of the archetypes in the collective unconscious had parallels in their own esoteric domains. Therefore the word 'archetype' has come to be used outside its strict Jungian sense to convey the idea of structures of spiritual forces woven into our inner souls. These archetypes are the shadows of spiritual forces embedded in the soul's structure. The esoteric tradition would describe these as being spiritual patterns woven into our astral bodies. This is a more radical change in meaning than at first it may appear. The difference imported with this esoteric interpretation of the archetype is that it has 'being' behind it. Jung saw the archetypes as arising out of the past experience of the race, and at least in print always kept to this strict view. This allowed his psychological theories to remain within the mainstream of the agnostic, skeptical, academic tradition, although Jung may have privately held a more immanent view of the archetypes which he kept for off-the-record conversations with his disciples.

So I use the word 'archetype' in this book to mean those spiritual patterns woven into our astral soul, as the embodiment of spiritual being in our inner substance. This may be a difficult idea for many of us to understand, so perhaps I can illustrate it in the following way. If archetypes are merely the husks of old racial memories writ large in the psyche, then we can only relate to them by trying to free ourselves of the forces bound up in them. This is indeed a valid approach, and that pursued in Jungian analysis, where patients are enabled to become conscious of and realize the energies of these archetypes working in their souls. However, the esotericist sees these archetypes not as the psychic garbage of a previous age, but as the reflection of spiritual being in our souls. Esotericists feel they should instead relate to these archetypes as being immanent with spiritual forces which eternally renew themselves in our souls. Through these archetypes we can experience a living relationship to the spiritual in ourselves. The archetypes are full of being to the esotericist. One can see the great distance that actually lies between these two conceptions of 'archetype.'

The esotericist working today can relate to these archetypes as the seat of spiritual being in our souls, eternally woven into the fabric of our astral bodies by the spiritual forces. In this sense we bear the 'Gods' within our being, rather than projecting them outside ourselves onto the material world, onto the Sky with its planets and stars, the Earth with her mountains, springs and deep clefts, or the living world of Nature as spirits of trees and vegetation, or onto totemic animals. In ancient times the Gods were seen in the world outside of us; now our consciousness has so grown and developed that instead we have come to see the Gods within our souls manifesting as archetypes.

The Gods cannot manifest in our intellect. They can only embody themselves in the astral substance of our being which remains free from the hardening forces of the material world and allows their spiritual energies to weave structures fluid enough to reflect their subtle spiritual nature.

The archetypes are woven into our astral substance, and thus we cannot expect to raise them into the more rigid substance of our abstract thinking, with its one-dimensional logical ordering of component ideas. The spiritual energies of the archetypes cannot live in such rigid structures. If we want to connect with the being of these spiritual impulses, it is pointless to hope that we can raise them into our abstract consciousness and examine them like bright jewels or pretty pictures; rather we have to go down into our inner world and make a meeting with them.

How are we to meet with these archetypes?

We have to be prepared to undertake an inner

journey. It is easy to throw oneself headlong into this experience by using certain extreme spiritual exercises taught in some magical groups or by the use of a variety of hallucinogenic drugs, or even by actively creating in oneself a state bordering upon madness. All of these methods will certainly propel us abruptly into the unconscious mind. However, the important thing about embarking upon an inner journey is not necessarily to achieve the end of the journey immediately. It is rather the quality of insight we have while traveling in this inner landscape, and what we are able to bring back into our everyday consciousness and outer life from such a journey. We cannot expect to live in an eternal, ecstatic, meditative state, nor eternally 'high' on some drug, and a constant state of psychic breakdown is hardly a valid life experience.

To gain anything from a journey we must make adequate preparation. The first level of working with these archetypes is to prepare our abstract thinking (the starting point from which we all begin our inner journeys), making it more flexible and able to reflect spiritual energies. It is my hope that some of the material in this book will assist with this. I have tried here to present some of this mythological material in a way which resonates with the archetypes and yet builds bridges toward them from our abstract thinking.

We begin then by contemplating the archetypal figures in our souls from the safe ground of our abstract everyday consciousness, and although we initially stand outside them, we will find that as we allow them to work upon us a dialogue or conversation begins to form itself. If we listen to our inner world, conscious of the fact that the archetypes dwelling there possess being and are not merely pretty intellectual toys, we will in time make a relationship with these foundation stones in our souls.

For those among the readers of this book who wish

to work further with the substance of this book, you should set aside some time to regularly contemplate these Goddess figures, say, just for example, the Erinyes. First you will have to read all the available relevant myths and legends connected with the Erinyes, not as an academic study but just to drink in the essence of the mythic material surrounding these archetypes. Try to gain an inner picture of what reveals itself through this archetype, the furious, jealous, guardian element of this facet of the Triple Goddess, and her primal uncompromising qualities. Try to see her in yourself. Examine whether you have ever reacted to situations or people in a way that is reminiscent of an Erinyes. All of us have at some time. Try to see this in others, or in group situations manifested in politics or social matters. If you try to build consciously an inner picture and seek out the Erinyes side of yourself, you will in time begin to feel her shape within you, as if this archetype were a solid element, a foundation stone within your soul. Of course, you would not focus exclusively on one facet of the Triple Goddess, but balance these exercises by experiencing the other sides of the Goddess as well.

All esoteric exercises begin with such simple everyday states of consciousness. The secret of inner development and spiritual experience lies in the will to pursue this task and not in some elaborate system of meditation. Balance is important, however, and we should avoid focusing on one facet of the Goddess which we might happily prefer to empathize with. (The same strictures apply when working with masculine Gods.) It is more important to connect with the different facets of the archetypes, to recognize their interaction and feel that the free flow of their qualities in our souls is essential to a healthy balance of our psychic energies. One can see quite clearly how the one-pointed focus upon the masculine Christ figure in the spiritual tradition of the West has led to an imbalance in the soul of Western humanity. We have to avoid repeating such errors in our inner work. Indeed, the whole point of this book focusing upon the Triple Goddess archetype is to provide people with some understanding of the need for inner balance, which I believe we can see quite clearly is woven into her spiritual substance.

If we pursue such exercises, in time we will begin to see that our inner response to people, events and situations reflects facets of the Triple Goddess, and once we are well acquainted with her we will note how we project a particular archetype upon certain individuals. This ongoing communication with the archetypes of our being is an important and essential part of the process, though only after having worked in this way for some years will it be possible for a more direct encounter with the spiritual energies bound up in these archetypes to take place. We have to prepare ourselves for the journey.

This direct encounter involves meditative work. Although several esoteric schools give instruction and supervise the practice of such inner workings, it is not essential for each individual to work through such groups. In a strange way, those who begin the process of preparing for their inner journey and work to transmute their abstract thinking into a valid vehicle for experiencing the archetypes will find that such meditative exercises spontaneously arise in them. When the time is right, and they have achieved a certain openness and flexibility in their thinking, the spiritual energies of the archetypes they have been working with will begin to flow into their consciousness. Such a state can only be gained through active work and long preparation. We must have the patience to wait upon the archetype of the Goddess in the soul to speak to us. She cannot be taken by storm.

Now many people have difficulties in working with Goddess energies and become frightened of certain archetypes, particularly of the Hag, Hecate,

Lilith or the Witch figure. I believe this arises purely out of projecting the patriarchal values in the form of dualism into their esoteric work. Once the Triple Goddess is recognized in her totality through her three facets simultaneously it is obvious that there is no dualism; there is no battle of 'good' and 'evil' in the soul. The Hag element is simultaneously the wise woman, the Sophia. To work with Goddess archetypes is indeed a powerful lesson in facing up to and overcoming the dualistic values imported into our souls through millennia of patriarchal dualism. So we need not fear the 'dark' side of the Goddess. She has her own beauty wrapped within her black cloak. Light, after all, depends on darkness for its being. We all need this dark planet for our nourishment as much as we need the bright Sun. We all need the dark unconscious realm within us as a fount of inspiration, surprise, and transformation, as much as we need the solid, secure, logical building blocks of our conscious mind.

If esotericists work in an exclusively patriarchal tradition they experience great difficulties in achieving this inner experience of their dark side. For in a patriarchal system the dark side of the soul is seen as entirely 'evil,' 'demonic,' 'satanic,' while the light side is wholly 'good' and 'spiritual.' The masculine God forms that are associated with the dark side, 'Pan,' 'Dionysus,' 'Satan,' and with profound contradiction 'Lucifer' (the 'light bringer'), have over the millennia of patriarchy been overlaid with such negative elements that it is almost impossible for an esotericist today to unite polarities using these masculine archetypes, so charged have they come to be with negative dualistic energies. The Triple Goddess remains a much healthier archetype to work with if we wish to unite the dark and light sides of our being, for, as we have seen, she synthesizes the polarities through the integrity of her triple nature. Working with the Triple Goddess is not fraught with the same dangers of dualistic projection as those which lie on the path of working through masculine archetypes.

I would like, in conclusion, to deal further with the question of the balance of the masculine and feminine and the seeming unbalanced focus of this present book on the feminine. As I indicated in my introduction, the human soul is already unbalanced, tipped heavily towards the masculine. This book is an attempt to provide some material that might help to redress this balance. If it was pursued exclusively as a path in itself, a working with only the Goddess side of our nature would eventually have unbalancing and distorting effects on the soul. However, there is such a mass of masculine components already woven into our souls that it would be a long time before an overbalance towards the feminine would result. So I make no apology for encouraging people to seek the feminine components of their inner nature.

I am aware that some people might think it presumptuous of me, as a man, to write on the Goddess or feminine component of the spirit and soul. Those who read this book more deeply will, I trust, come to see that 'masculine' and 'feminine' are not inextricably bound up with our physiological sex, but live in our souls which are not sexually differentiated. We are all 'human' in our souls, not 'masculine' or 'feminine'; we ensoul both components. Indeed, in this present book I argue that it is the polarization of patriarchy that has brought about the illusion that our souls are sexually differentiated. One branch of the early Protestant movement went so far as to declare that women's souls were so inferior to men's that it was impossible for them to enter the kingdom of heaven—who indeed would want to enter such a distorted heaven anyway, one is tempted to wonder. Because of this illusion, this grand lie, men have been forced to repress the feminine component of their inner nature and women their masculine side if they were to survive and succeed in a patriarchal society.

So although I do not feel I have intruded upon an exclusively women's territory in writing of the Goddess (who belongs to us all), this present book is a view of the Triple Goddess seen from a masculine perspective. Any insights I have into this material have arisen through my touching upon the feminine realm within myself. I do not doubt that a different view and experience would arise if a woman were to write on the same subject, but I hope I have touched upon sufficiently universal ground to make the material of value and relevance for future studies or individual experiences of the archetype of the Triple Goddess.

There are differences in the ways in which men and women can relate to the Triple Goddess. Men see her reflected in the feminine side of their souls. Although they can perceive her as a psychic structure within their beings through which certain energies can manifest, there is almost always in men an element of separation, of standing apart from this Triple Goddess archetype within their souls. Men can rarely unite with this archetype, and therefore are rarely inwardly overwhelmed by such a feminine archetype, though they can get into difficulties by projecting a facet of it upon some individual woman. It often happens that men are overwhelmed, overshadowed, and become obsessed by uniting their beings with a masculine archetype. We have all seen men who see themselves as 'saviors,' being overwhelmed by a 'Christ' or 'hero' archetype, usually only for a few short years before this inner identification with the archetype begins to dissolve. So, although there are dangers in relating to archetypes, rarely are men able to step inside the Triple Goddess in the way that they are able to do so with masculine spiritual forms. Since there is little danger of identifying with the Triple Goddess figure, she can become, for men, a safe inner guide to their souls.

For women the case is different. The Triple Goddess lives in the active side of a woman's psyche, and women are constantly having to identify with and work though one of her facets. It is therefore vitally important that women gain insight into and understanding of all facets of the Goddess and the ways in which she manifests in their beings. Otherwise they are not free in their souls, but are likely to be overwhelmed or pressed into certain facets of the Goddess in response to situations. Thus a woman might find herself bound up in a certain facet of the Goddess without necessarily exercising her will in a manner reflecting free choice. She may, for example, become overwhelmed by the Siren aspect, and devote almost all her time, life's energy, and potential to projecting sexual allure in an attempt to attract men to her. Similarly, she may become entirely given up to the Mother facet and sacrifice other aspects of her soul to working through her family. The Crone or wise-woman facet can also fascinate certain women, who thus come to see themselves as having special insight or intuition into the events of life, often so needing to express this inner archetypal identification that they meddle and interfere in the lives of others. Women have to step into the Triple Goddess, and the dangers for them lie in a one sided development of a particular facet of the archetype.

A conscious understanding of the Goddess in her wholeness is an important inner psychic tool for women to employ in order to experience the energies flowing in their souls. So many women, being unconscious of the structural elements in their psyches, are rather at the mercy of whatever facet of the Goddess is active within them. Often such archetypal identifications are sparked off by forces outside their beings, by pressures from outer society and traditional 'roles.' Sometimes their husbands, partners, or families project a particular facet of the archetype onto them. Even the pressure of the media, plays, and advertising impress themselves strongly into the psyche. All of these many pressures seek to mold women and make them conform at different times in their lives to certain archetypes.

So it must be of the greatest importance for women who wish to have some control over their inner lives, and consequently their outer expression and potentiality in society, to have an understanding of the power and architecture of the Triple Goddess within them.

Men have a triple facet also, which I have alluded to in my earlier book on the Four Fire Festivals. That work discusses the feminine earthly cycle of seasonal festivals particularly associated with Celtic peoples. The male psyche bears within itself a reflection of the Triple Goddess. Thus we have Man the Warrior: the heroic, exploratory, investigative aspect of the male, a remnant of a Hunter archetype, this young knight or hero corresponding to the Maiden aspect of the Goddess. Next we can recognize Man the Husband: the protective, guardian aspect of the man, earning his living and supporting wife and children, providing for and nourishing the next generation. This is a remnant of man the agriculturalist, partner to the Mother facet of the Goddess. The third facet is Man the Creator, man in the role of artist, musician, poet, sculptor, or writer, in which men open themselves to the promptings of inspiration to create and bring new ideas, art and inventions into the world. This complements the Crone or wise-woman facet of the Goddess. In this way men bear within themselves a triple aspect with which they have to identify. Many men have great inner difficulty in facing up to the implications of working through a particular role or of repressing and denying one of these facets of themselves; this parallels the problems of inner identification women have in relating to facets of the Goddess. Similarly, women find that these three facets of the male archetype—Knight, Husband, and Artist—are woven into the masculine side of themselves. If they reflect these inwardly and try to explore the qualities of this triplicity and its relationship to the triplicity of the Goddess archetype within them, they will gain a greater understanding of their relationship to the masculine.

An awareness of this facet of our beings can be the beginning of a process of inner communication, meeting, and eventual conjunction and flowing together of these male and female triplicities in our souls. If the soul is able to work freely with these forces within itself and unite the polarities in an inner alchemical fusion—a dynamic meeting of the opposites—then the individual soul is able to become truly human. It can encompass, in a balanced way, all the masculine and feminine forces within itself. There can be no more important task for humanity than this. If we could collectively achieve such a state of inner development, we could indeed claim to be fully human and could hold our spiritual essence and potential within our grasp.

I do hope that this book might help a little in encouraging people to relate to the feminine components of their inner nature and to embark upon the great inner alchemical process of reconciling and conjoining the Opposites—the inner Alchemical Marriage.

PHANES PRESS both publishes and distributes many fine books which relate to the philosophical, religious and spiritual traditions of the Western world. To obtain a copy of our current catalogue, please write:

PHANES PRESS
PO BOX 6114
GRAND RAPIDS, MI 49516
USA